This book belongs to:

....

Authors Andrea Mills, Lizzie Munsey
Subject Consultant Jean Menzies
Editor Abi Luscombe
Project Editor Sophie Parkes
Senior Art Editor Claire Patane
Project Art Editors Victoria Palastanga, Bhagyashree Nayak
Designers Hannah Moore, Sadie Thomas, Karen Hood
Additional editorial Nate Rae, Clare Lloyd, Rea Pikula, Anna Bonnerjea
Additional design Ann Cannings, Brandie Tully-Scott, Sonny Flynn, Eleanor Bates
Additional illustrations Kitty Glavin, Mohd Zishan, Priyal Mote
Senior Picture Researcher Sakshi Saluja
Managing Editor Penny Smith
Production Editor Becky Fallowfield
Senior Production Controller Inderjit Bhullar
Jacket Designers Claire Patane, Sadie Thomas
Jacket Coordinator Elin Woosnam
Art Director Mabel Chan
Managing Director Sarah Larter

First published in Great Britain in 2024 by
Dorling Kindersley Limited
DK, One Embassy Gardens, 8 Viaduct Gardens,
London, SW11 7BW

The authorised representative in the EEA is
Dorling Kindersley Verlag GmbH. Arnulfstr. 124,
80636 Munich, Germany

A CIP catalogue record for this book
is available from the British Library.
ISBN: 978-0-2415-8496-5

Printed and bound in China

www.dk.com

MIX
Paper | Supporting
responsible forestry
FSC™ C018179

This book was made with Forest
Stewardship Council™ certified
paper – one small step in DK's
commitment to a sustainable future.
Learn more at
www.dk.com/uk/information/sustainability

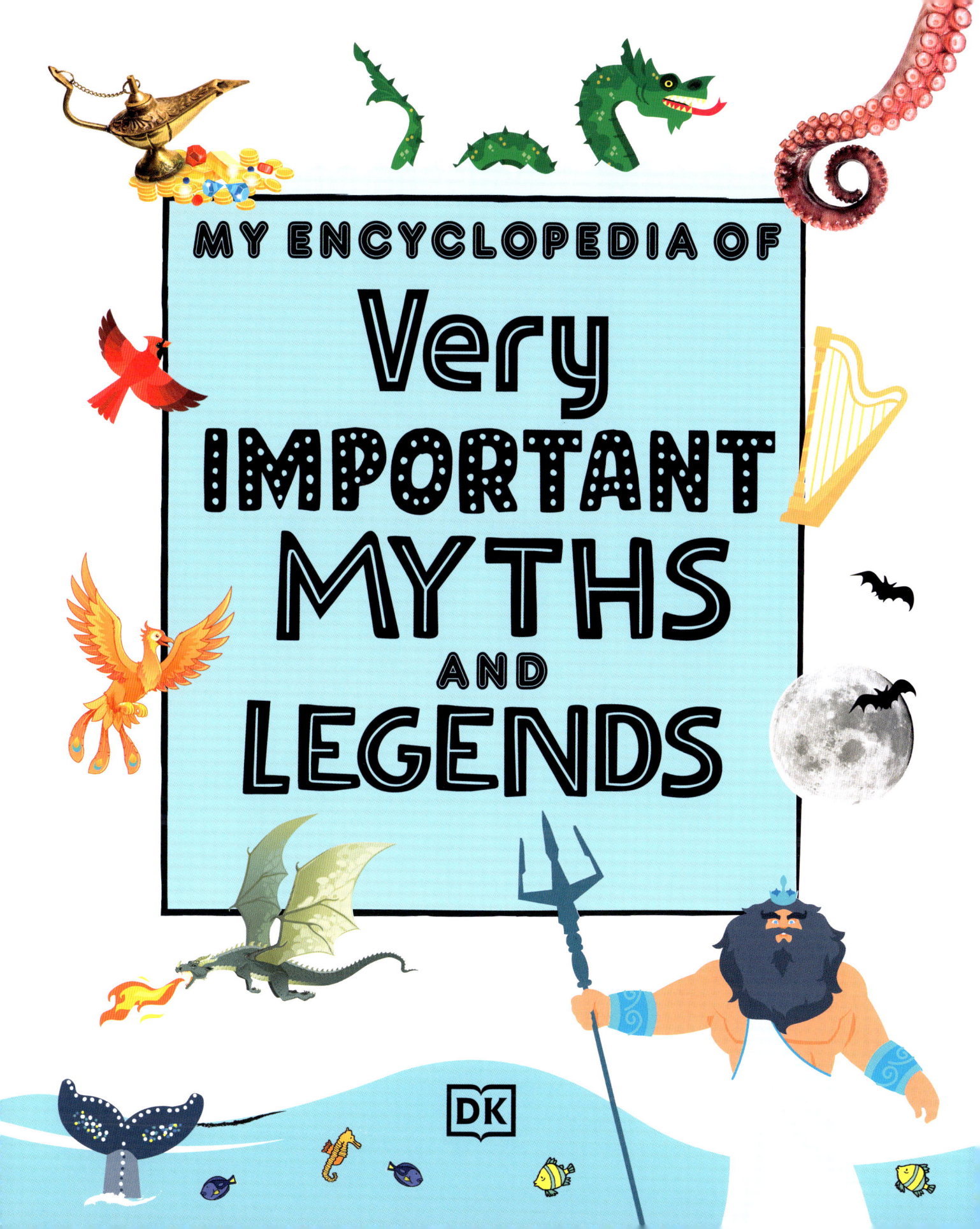

MY ENCYCLOPEDIA OF
Very
IMPORTANT
MYTHS
AND
LEGENDS

DK

Contents

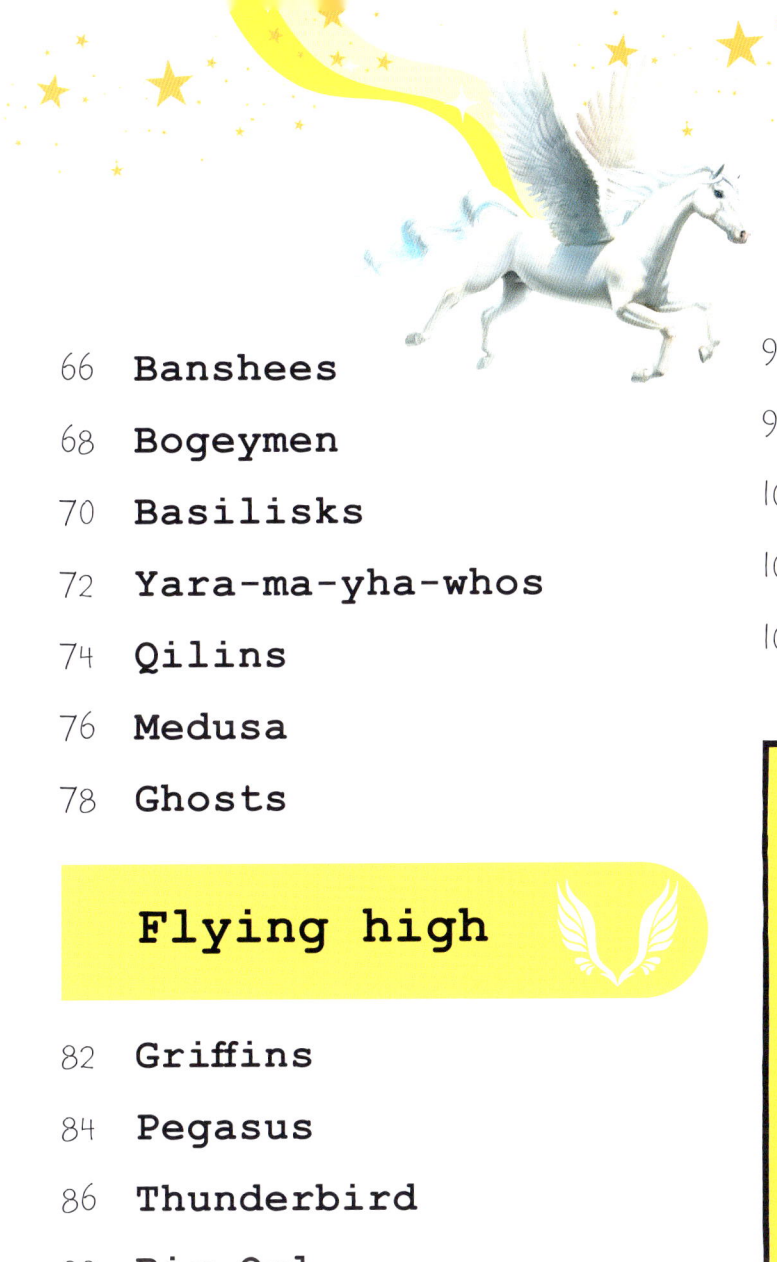

A note for readers

A myth is a story that explains history and tends to feature magical beings. A legend is a mythical story from the past that tells of a famous event or action. Each myth and legend in this book is just one version of many. Different people, cultures, and religions may view these stories differently and many have changed over time. Some of the myths and legends in this book are sacred and reflect the beliefs of people in the past and present.

Magic and mischief

Heroes and battles

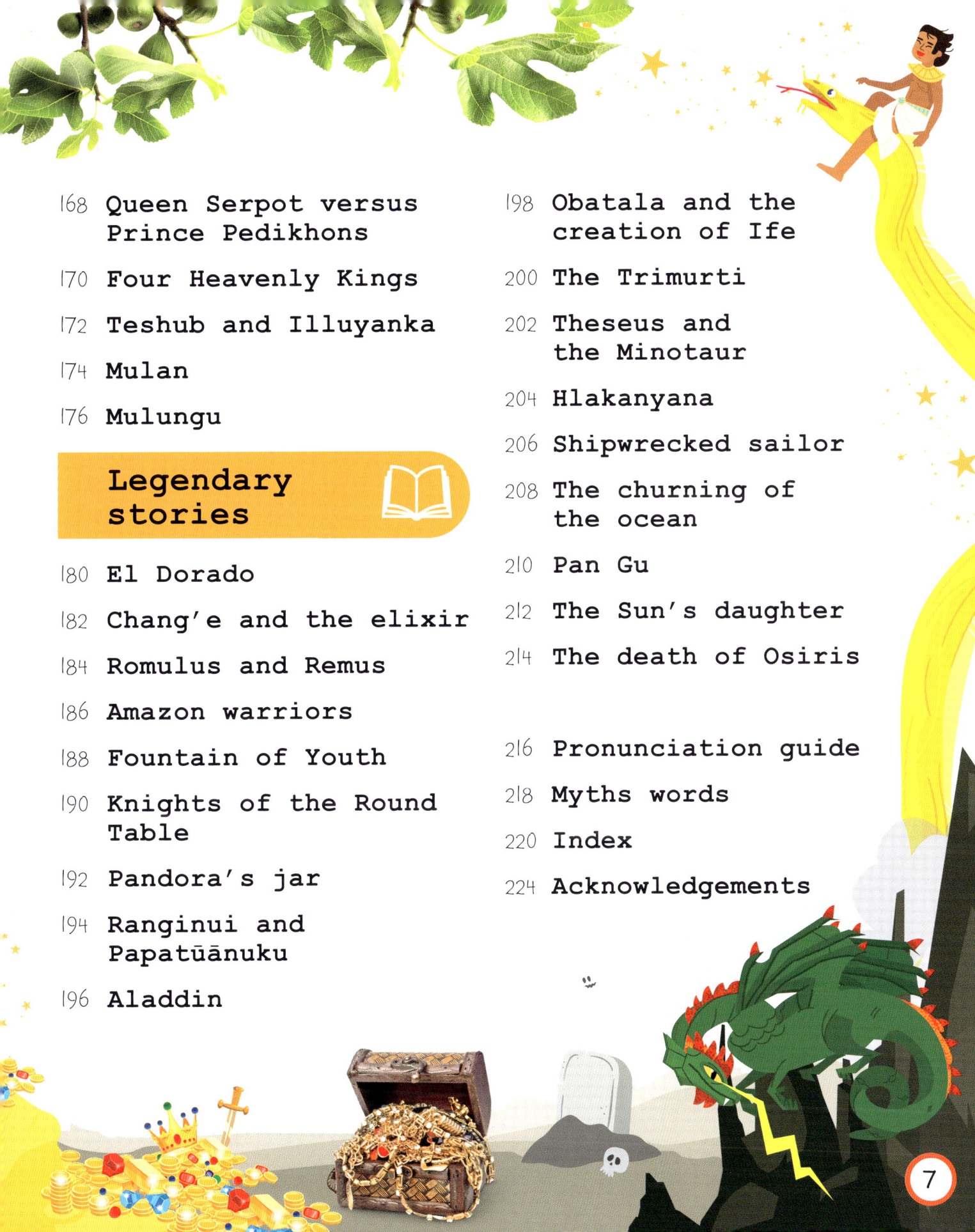

Legends of the **water**

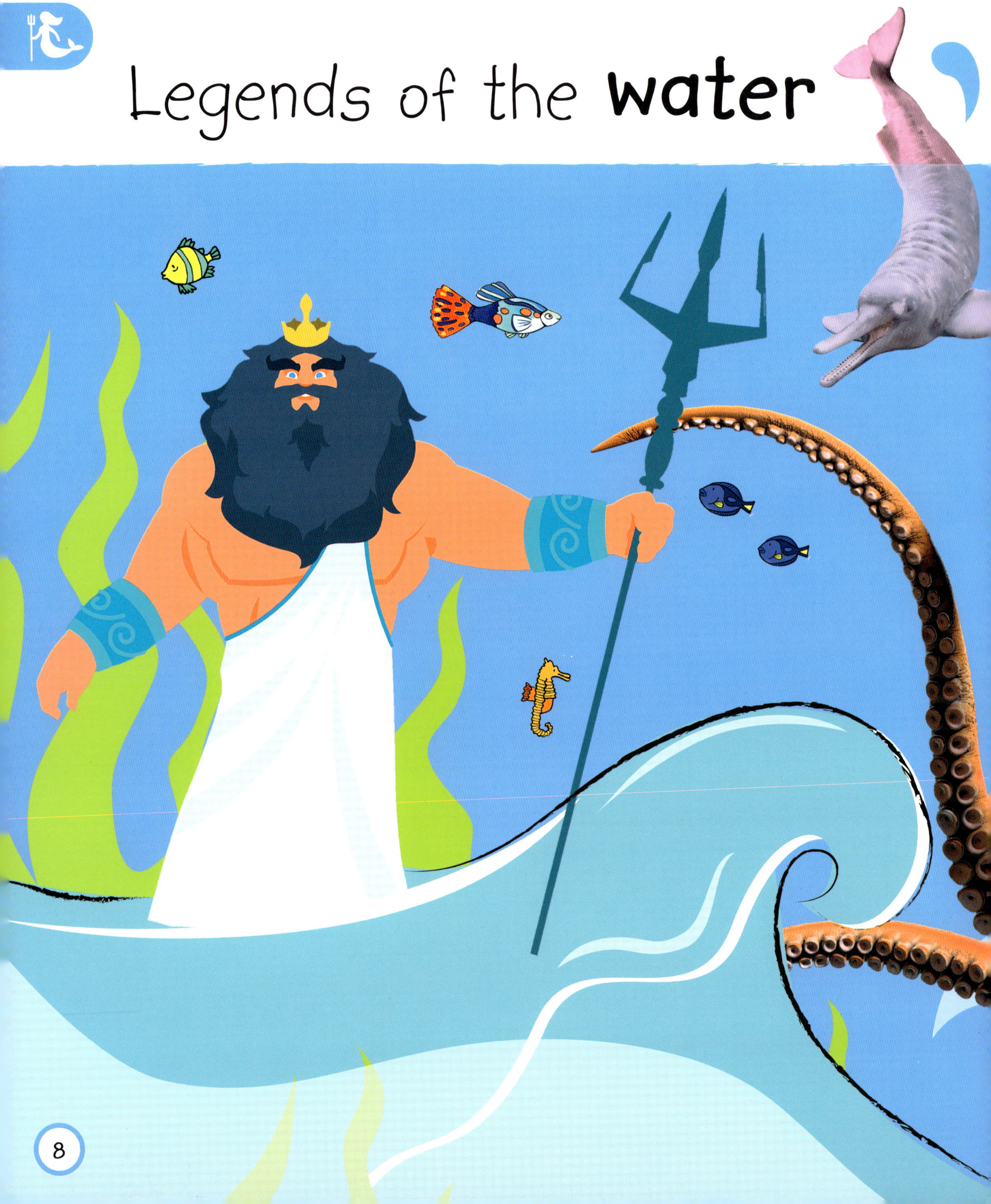

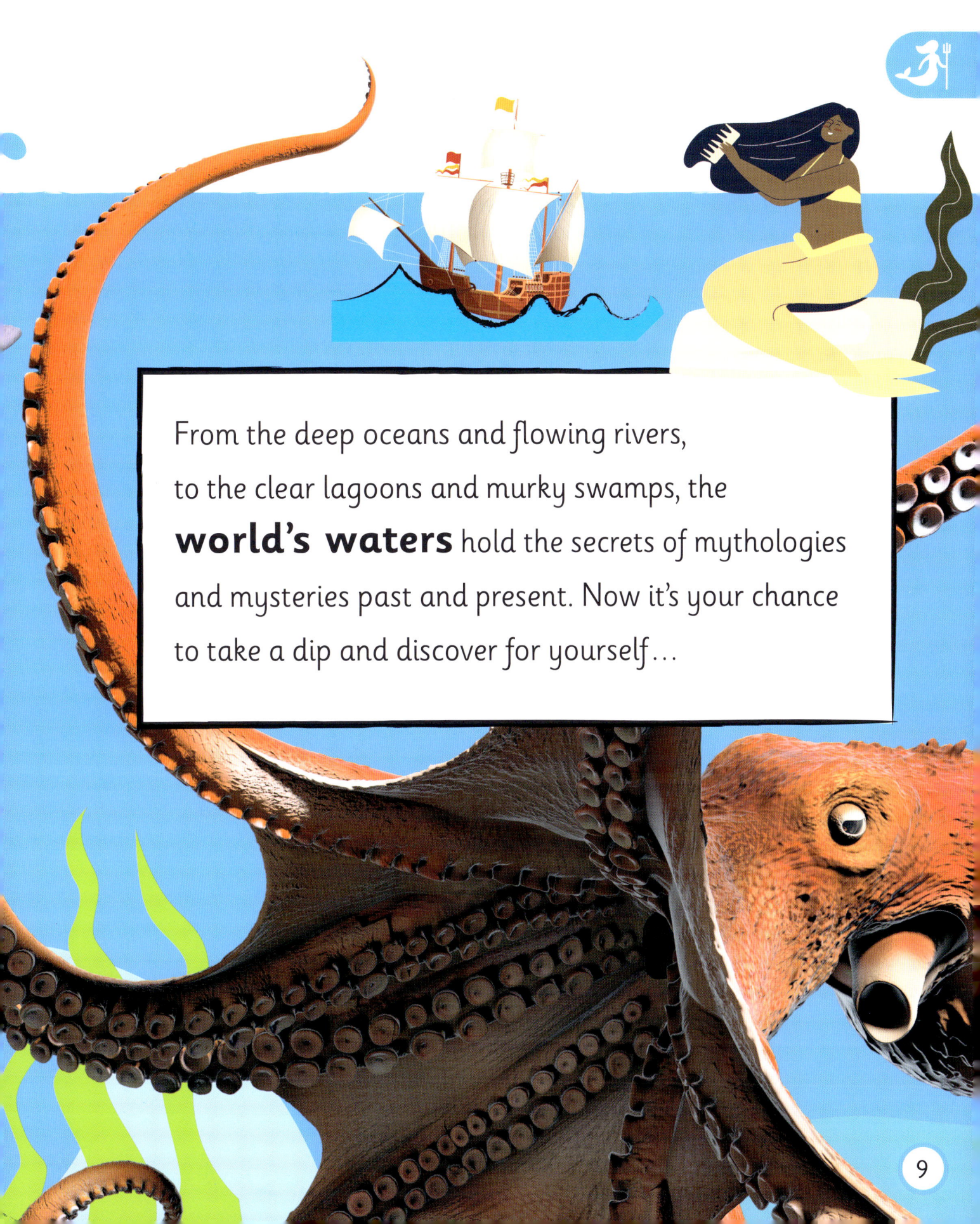

From the deep oceans and flowing rivers, to the clear lagoons and murky swamps, the **world's waters** hold the secrets of mythologies and mysteries past and present. Now it's your chance to take a dip and discover for yourself…

Atlantis

Legend goes that beneath the ocean waves lies a mysterious kingdom that **sank** without a trace in ancient times. Experts have been looking for it ever since…

…in a single day and night of misfortune, the island of Atlantis disappeared into the depths of the sea.

Plato

Underwater island

In about 360 BCE, Greek philosopher Plato described a stunning island called **Atlantis** that existed 9,000 years before him. Here, people lived happily until a disaster left it lost underwater. Whether due to a huge earthquake or a giant tsunami, the island vanished completely.

According to Plato's writings, those who

Plato's story got many people thinking – where was Atlantis and could it ever be found? Scientists used new technologies to explore the seas and try to find this legendary place.

Finding Atlantis

Many different places have been suggested as the location for Atlantis. Here are just a few of them:

Spain
Marshes in southern Spain flooded thousands of years ago. Satellite images led to one theory that the city walls of Atlantis had been found.

Santorini
As in the story of Atlantis, the Greek island of Santorini was devastated by disaster. A volcanic eruption in about 1613 BCE ruined the island and the civilizations living there.

Bimini Road
In 1938, an American fortune teller declared that Atlantis lay underwater at Bimini Road, a formation of strange stones near the Bahamas.

Bermuda Triangle
The Bermuda Triangle is an area in the Atlantic Ocean where boats and planes have disappeared. Was Atlantis also swallowed up by the Bermuda Triangle?

Poseidon

According to ancient Greek folklore, Poseidon, god of the sea, built the city of Atlantis on a remote island out at sea. This was a **safe haven** for the love of his life, a woman named Cleito.

lived in Atlantis were HALF HUMAN and HALF GOD.

The kraken

Deep beneath the ocean waves lies a giant, **tentacled** monster – the kraken. If disturbed, it rises up to the ocean's surface, and pulls ships and sailors down to their doom.

Greenland

Norway

Freezing home

The kraken lives in the icy waters between **Greenland** and **Norway**.

Its existence was first suggested by Norse and Viking sailors...

...who sailed the seas...

...more than a thousand years ago.

Fish rising up from the depths of the ocean could

Scary squid

The kraken has a wide, beak-like mouth and sucker-covered tentacles. Its legend may have grown from sightings of **giant squid**, real animals that can grow up to 14 m (46 ft) long.

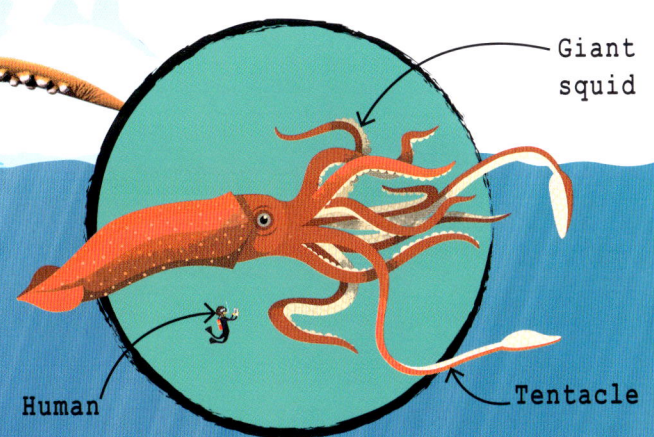

Giant squid

Human

Tentacle

Shrinking monster

Early stories about the kraken talk of a huge sea monster, which could be as big as an **island**. Over time the kraken seems to have shrunk – later stories describe it as closer to the size of a **ship**, but still completely terrifying.

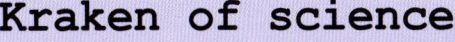

Kraken of science

In 1735, Swedish biologist **Carl Linnaeus** classified the kraken as a living thing, and even gave it a scientific name: *Microcosmus marinus*. However, he later had to remove it from his book due to lack of evidence.

Carl Linnaeus at work

Do not disturb!

If left alone, the kraken is not dangerous. However, if it is disturbed by a ship, then **beware** – the kraken awakes! It rises from the seabed, ready to take its anger out on anything close by.

LOOK OUT!

be a sign that the kraken is ON ITS WAY.

Sirens

If you are sailing near rocky cliffs and hear a bewitching song – beware! The **ancient Greeks** believed women called sirens lived here. They sang to lure sailors to their deaths.

Siren song

Sometimes sirens are described as beings with the **bodies of women** and the **legs and wings of birds**. Other times they are described as normal women. Their singing was beautiful, and they played instruments such as harps and lyres.

Greek myths say that sirens lived on

Rocky death

Sirens lived in caves along rocky coastlines. On hearing the music of the sirens, **sailors** would do **anything** to hear it better. As they got near, they would smash their ships, jump overboard to get closer, and die.

Ship full of sailors

Odysseus and the sirens

The hero Odysseus wanted to hear the sirens' song. Before sailing past the sirens' roost, he told his crew to pack their ears with **wax** and then tie him to the **mast**. They only released him once they had passed the danger.

Nymphs

In Greek mythology, sirens are not the only water-dwelling women. Nymphs are female spirits who live in nature. Two types of nymphs live in water: **naiads** and **nereids**.

Naiads live in freshwater. They take care of rivers, lakes, and streams. Every major spring and river is said to have had at least one naiad living in it!

Nereids are sea nymphs. There are 50 of them, and they are daughters of the Titan Nereus, the "Old Man of the Sea". Nereids can be helpful to sailors by calming the sea.

rocks near a monster called SCYLLA.

Kappas

According to **Japanese** legend, the rivers and ponds of Japan are home to kappas – turtle-like spirits with magical powers.

Source of power

A kappa has a large, bowl-like dent on its head known as a **sara**, which means "dish" in Japanese. The kappa must keep the sara filled with water, as that is the source of its magical powers.

Turtle terror

A kappa is a child-sized turtle with a shell on its back. It has **slimy green skin**, a beak-like mouth, and webbed feet.

A friendly kappa might teach

In Japan, bowing when you meet someone is a sign of respect.

Outsmarting a kappa

The key to escaping a kappa is to **empty the water** from its sara, so it loses its power. Famed for its wrestling skills, a kappa is hard to beat in a fight. But it is also a very polite creature – if you bow to it, it will bow back, spilling the water from its head. If you then refill the sara, restoring the kappa's power, it will be a friend for life.

A cucumber sushi roll is called "KAPPA MAKI" in Japan.

Magic powers

As well as having magic powers, the kappa is intelligent and **mischievous**. It will combine its powers and cunning to play nasty tricks on people or lure them into dangerous water where it can attack.

Share your greens

A kappa's favourite food is **cucumber**. People give cucumbers as offerings to kappas at Japanese festivals.

you how to MEND broken bones.

Ra and the Sun

The **ancient Egyptians** worshipped the Sun god Ra, believing his dazzling daily journey across the sky was the source of all light and life on Earth.

Sun worshippers

Many ancient cultures worshipped the Sun. In Egypt, the Sun god Ra had the head of a **falcon** and a symbolic Sun disk on his headdress.

By day

Every morning at sunrise, Ra appeared in his burning boat, called **Mandjet**. He travelled across the heavens until sunset.

Ra sailing in Mandjet

Ra is the Egyptian word for "Sun".

DAY

Ancient Egyptians believed that the first people in

Underworld, here I come!

Ra sailing in Mesektet

By night

At night, Ra then boarded his other boat, **Mesektet**, and sailed into the underworld. It was thought that it was dark at night because Ra had gone to the world of the dead.

Under attack

Every night, Ra faced a battle in the underworld. The giant serpent **Apep** wanted to stop the Sun rising and end life on Earth. But Ra chopped off his head.

Ra defeating Apep

NIGHT

The Great Pyramids of Giza at sunrise

Endless journey

After battle, Ra emerged at daybreak to bring light to the world. He travelled **24 hours** a day and faced his serpent enemy every time.

the world were created from the TEARS OF RA.

Qallupilluit

According to **Inuit** mythology, scary sea creatures patrol the icy Arctic waters. They have deadly intentions, but their story is shared for good reasons.

Warning signs

For centuries, the Inuit people of Alaska and Canada have described monsters in the deep. They say there are signs to watch out for. The sulphur smell of **rotten eggs** suggests qallupilluit are close by. A low humming noise is their siren call.

Once seen, never forgotten

Picture a beautiful mermaid – and then imagine the complete opposite! Qallupilluit have **bedraggled hair**, **slimy skin**, and **sunken eyes**. They have webbed feet and hands for swimming, with sharp claws for snatching.

Doom and gloom

It is said that qallupilluit try to steal children. They lure them to the shoreline by **humming** before jumping out of the water and grabbing them between their claws. Children have no chance of escape and are **pulled underwater** to their doom.

Survival story

The tale of the qallupilluit is told to teach children how to **stay safe**, where there is ocean and ice all around. By warning about qallupilluit, kids stay away from the water's edge, don't step on thin ice, and avoid the risk of drowning.

Invit mothers wear big coats, called amautiit, which have *built-in baby* pouches – and *so do* the child-snatching qallupilluit.

Qalupalik amauti

Amauti

Hydra

This colossal water snake terrorized the people of **ancient Greece**. Its story is told as part of the myth of a famous Greek hero, called Heracles.

Endless heads

The Hydra had an impressive **nine** heads! If one of its heads was cut off, two more instantly grew to take its place. The Hydra's central head was also said to be **immortal**, which means that it couldn't be killed.

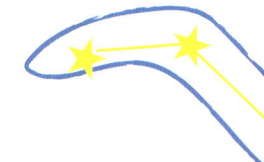

Dangerous creature

It wasn't just the heads that made the Hydra dangerous. The animal's **entire body was toxic**: its breath was poisonous gas, and its blood was so dangerous that anyone who touched it **would die instantly**.

The Hydra lived in a lake near Lerna, Greece. The gates to the underworld were under this lake, and the Hydra guarded them. When it left the lake, it rampaged across the countryside, killing people and causing a lot of damage.

There is a snake-shaped **CONSTELLATION** named after the Hydra.

Hydra star constellation

Hydra

Iolaus

Heracles

Death of the Hydra

Many people tried and failed to kill the Hydra, until **Heracles** eventually managed it. As he cut off each head, his nephew **Iolaus** burned the leftover stump, **stopping new heads** from growing. Heracles killed the final, immortal head with a magical sword.

Heracles with his magical sword

Maman Dlo

This **Caribbean water spirit** protects the islands' flowing rivers and tropical seas. She even encourages new recruits to join her underwater!

Mythical mermaid

The name Maman Dlo means "**mother of the water**". She is an older lady, usually shown with the long hair and fish-like tail associated with **mermaids**.

Mother nature

Maman Dlo looks after the water and its wildlife. She also **guides sailors** safely through storms and **punishes anyone polluting** the seas and rivers. She is a **great healer** who can treat any illnesses that come from bad water.

Ti Jeanne's tale

One day, a young village girl named Ti Jeanne waded into the river to do her laundry. She sang to herself as she washed the clothing. Suddenly, from under the water, a strange hissing voice asked who was there. The voice of Maman Dlo enchanted Ti Jeanne and she fell under Maman Dlo's spell.

Hiss hiss

Spirited away

Ti Jeanne found herself underwater with Maman Dlo where her hair grew long and her legs were replaced by a fish tail. She had become a water spirit, too! Forever more, she was Mamam Dlo's faithful servant, helping her to care for the waters.

Great escape

The villagers came out looking for Ti Jeanne and found only her laundry basket left on the riverbank. To avoid the same fate, it is said you should remove your left shoe, turn it upside down, and leave it by the water — then walk all the way home backwards.

Leviathan

Colossal in size and massively strong, Leviathan is an ancient sea serpent that rules the ocean depths. It appears in many stories from the **Middle East**.

Some stories about Leviathan say that it might have...

Biblical beast

The Hebrew and Christian Bibles tell of the monster Leviathan being **killed by God**. Once it was dead, God gave it to his people as food. Leviathan was massive, so it would have made meals for a great many people.

Today, the word "leviathan" is used to describe things that are monstrously big!

Boiling breath

Leviathan has scorching **breath**, hot enough to **boil seawater** and create clouds of **steam**. It can even breathe fire, and smoke pours out of its nostrils. Some stories tell that Leviathan's superheated breath is also extremely **smelly**.

...as many as SEVEN HEADS!

Help!

Help!

Help!

Leviathan is so large that it eats the biggest creatures it can find: whales. Leviathan needs to eat an entire whale every single day.

Ship-swallower

Jewish folk stories describe Leviathan as a terrifying, dangerous monster of the seas. Leviathan can **swallow ships whole**, along with all the sailors on board. It **causes chaos** wherever it appears.

Scylla and Charybdis

In **Greek** mythology, Scylla and Charybdis were a **deadly duo** that terrorized a stretch of Mediterranean water, making it impossible for ships to pass safely.

Scylla

Supernatural Scylla

This supernatural, **many-headed beast** was a sight to behold! She lived in a cave by the ocean waiting to gobble up passing sailors with her **sharp teeth**. She also made a spine-chilling sound. Some tales claim Scylla was a nymph who was turned into a sea monster.

Terrifying team

Scylla and Charybdis worked in partnership, causing chaos in the narrow **Strait of Messina**. With Scylla patrolling one side and Charybdis on the other, it was impossible for ships to avoid one or the other.

Many Greek heroes came face to face with Scylla and Charybdis, including Odysseus, Heracles, and Jason and the Argonauts.

Chaotic Charybdis

In contrast, Charybdis was an unstoppable force of nature. This great **whirlpool** brought havoc to the ocean, churning up the waters to dangerous speeds. The swirl was so strong that it sucked ships underwater and down to their doom **three times a day**.

Charybdis

Difficult position

Sailors faced an **impossible choice**, which led to the saying "between Scylla and Charybdis". Today, a similar saying is "caught between a rock and a hard place".

Encantados

The Amazon River in **South America** is home to Amazon river dolphins. Legends say that you can also find Encantados —magical dolphin-like creatures that can take on human form.

Human dolphins
The Encantados are extremely **beautiful** and **graceful**. Their beauty makes them stand out from regular humans.

Encantado

Amazon river dolphin

Underwater heaven
The word Encantado means "enchanted one" in Portuguese. Many people in Brazil believe that the Encantados come from a heaven-like kingdom called the "**Encante**", which is hidden somewhere underwater.

People in Brazil have talked about

Dolphin blowhole

Hidden feature

Encantados have a blowhole on their head, causing a bald spot. To cover the hole when in human form, Encandatos often wear a **wide straw hat**.

Party animals

Encantados love parties and festivals with dancing and music, and are talented **musicians**. An Encantado can become the life and soul of a party, singing and dancing the night away.

Stolen friends

Sometimes, the Encantados kidnap people they might have **fallen in love** with. These unlucky humans are taken to the Amazon River, then underwater, to the Encante.

The Amazon River runs through three countries: Peru, Colombia, and Brazil.

the Encantados for **HUNDREDS** of years.

Dakuwaqa

Fijian folklore tells tales of the **shark god** Dakuwaqa, a ferocious and fearsome ruler of the waves.

Island icon

Fiji is a remote country made up of more than **300 islands** in the Pacific Ocean. Many local myths revolve around the ocean. Dakuwaqa is one of the **most famous**.

Yasawa Island, Fiji

Sea of change

Dakuwaqa is usually shown as **half-man**, **half-shark**, but he has the power to **shape-shift**. He can turn into any living thing and copy their characteristics, such as changing into a human and living on land!

Tokairahe's treasure

One day, Dakuwaqa came up against **Tokairahe**, god of fishermen. Tokairahe had a magical necklace of fishing hooks and shells, which gave him power over ocean life. The hooks swept through the water, **catching fish**.

Tokairahe

Biting back

Dakuwaqa wondered how he could **save the ocean** from Tokairahe. One morning, he saw Tokairahe wearing his magical necklace while diving. So Dakuwaqa swam underwater, snuck up on Tokairahe, and bit off the necklace with his razor-sharp teeth. Tokairahe's powers were gone.

It is said that anyone who insults Dakuwaqa gets eaten by a SHARK!

Guiding light

Dakuwaqa does many **heroic things**. Once, a local chief found himself in a storm at sea and his ship began sinking. The shark god emerged to guide the **ship to safety**, swimming with it all the way back to shore.

Water **spirits**

Lots of myths revolve around water spirits.
These magical beings controlled the oceans, rivers,
lakes, and streams – and often **caused chaos**!

Mami Wata

Known throughout **Africa**, Mami Wata is a powerful spirit, shown as **half-human** and **half-fish** or serpent. She tends to bring luck and fortune, but anyone who gets on the wrong side of her could end up being drowned!

Kāmohoali'i

Hawaiian god Kāmohoali'i is considered the king of all the sharks. People worship Kāmohoali'i, believing he can **calm the seas**. He is said to shape-shift into any fish and guide lost ships back to safety.

Rán

This **Norse goddess** rules the Scandinavian seas. She is typically shown with a **net** used to scoop up her victims and drown them!

Ryūjin

In **ancient Japanese** folklore, Ryūjin is a **dragon king** who lives in an underwater palace. He rules the tides and controls rainfall and thunderstorms. Local farmers set up shrines in his honour to encourage him to water their crops.

Chalchiuhtlicue

The **Aztec water goddess** was Chalchiuhtlicue. She is often shown carrying two babies as she is also the **goddess of birth**. It is believed her sacred waters could heal the sick.

Loch Ness monster

Legend says a mysterious monster lurks in the murky depths of Loch Ness in **Scotland**. People claim to have seen the creature, sometimes known as "Nessie", poking its head above the lake's surface.

"LOCH" is the Scottish word for a lake or ocean inlet.

Big beast

The Loch Ness monster has a long neck. It is said to be **huge** at 15 m (50 ft) – around the same length as a badminton court!

There are more than 1,100 recorded sightings of the Loch Ness monster.

Where's everyone gone?

Early sightings

Reports of a monstrous creature lurking in the loch date back as far as 565 CE. In one tale, a man is said to have been **attacked by a monster** while swimming. In another, a beast was reported to have jumped from the water and gobbled up a local farmer.

Prehistoric creature

Some people think that Nessie could be a **marine reptile** from the age of the dinosaurs, called a **plesiosaur**. However, plesiosaurs died out 66 million years ago with the dinosaurs.

Plesiosaurus skeleton

Monster hunting

In 1987 and 2003, people scanned the loch with **sonar**. They found no convincing proof of Nessie, but some fans believe she was **hiding**, as the loch reaches as deep as 230 m (755 ft).

Sonar uses sound waves to search for large objects.

The photo was exposed as a fake in 1994.

In 1934, an English newspaper published a photo of Nessie. It was said to be the first photograph of the monster.

Ganga

Followers of the **Hindu faith** worship the **Ganges River** as a goddess named Ganga. They believe her waters have the power to purify and forgive.

Goddess Ganga

Ganga is usually shown holding a **water lily** and a **vase**. She rides on the back of a crocodile-like creature called **makara**.

Holy river

The vast Ganges River flows through **India and Bangladesh**. All rivers are sacred in Hinduism, but this river is so important that it has been officially named India's national river.

Ganges River

Ganges and Yamuna rivers

Celestial creature

Ganga was once a **heavenly creature** who descended to Earth to help humankind. She came down to **save people** during a drought, and created the Ganges River. It is said the water she left behind in the sky can be seen as the Milky Way galaxy.

Come together

Hindu goddess Yamuna is the daughter of the Sun god and the cloud goddess. **Ganga** and **Yamuna** are often mentioned together because they are both also rivers in India. Yamuna flows into the Ganges, and the place where the rivers meet is a sacred site.

Hindus bathing in the Ganges River

Daily cleansing

Many Hindus bathe in the Ganges River every day because the water is considered **sacred**. Every New Year, Hindus wade through the Ganges to achieve health, protection, and to **wash away sins**.

One drop of Ganges water is said to erase a LIFETIME OF SINS.

Taniwha

In **Māori** mythology, there are stories that describe larger-than-life **lizards**. They can transform from terrifying monsters into protective guardians.

New Zealand

Taniwha in the form of a giant gecko.

Gleaming eyes

Māori monster

Taniwha are huge, **dragon-like creatures** typically covered in shiny, green scales. They light up the darkness with their gleaming eyes.

Watery wonders

Taniwha can take on different forms depending on their **environment**. They look more like **whales**, **sharks**, **or dolphins** in the ocean, or like giant **geckos** when in rivers. In other versions of the legend, anything goes! They can turn into floating logs or serpents, and can even fly with giant wings.

One of the worst taniwha was Tūtaeporoporo, a shark that hunted travellers on the river where he lived. He ate anyone he caught, and chomped through their canoes as well. When hero Ao-Kehu was sent to stop the taniwha, Tūtaeporoporo swallowed him whole! But Ao-Kehu cut himself out of Tūtaeporoporo's tummy, killing the taniwha for good.

Kupe

Safe passing

Many taniwha keep people **safe at sea**. The explorer Kupe was said to have a taniwha called Tuhirangi that protected him in his canoe. Taniwha have been said to save people from drowning at sea and warn sailors of deadly storms or dangerous waterfalls.

41

Mermaids

These water-loving creatures have the head, arms, and body of a woman, but their lower bodies are made up of something completely different – **a fish's tail**. Mermaids appear in stories from all over the world.

Incredible beauty

Mermaids are often described as extremely beautiful, with long, **flowing hair**. They are sometimes shown holding a mirror or a comb.

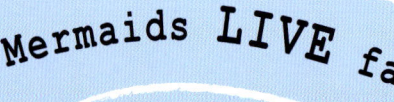

Mermaids LIVE far LONGER than humans do.

Dugong

Mermaid-like tail

People who claim to have seen mermaids might have actually spotted manatees or dugongs. These are both large mammals that live in the sea. Their lower halves look a little like a mermaid's tail, but their top halves are very different!

Danger to sailors

Mermaids sit on rocks, singing **beautiful songs**. However, their mermaid songs can be deadly. As the ships sail close to the mermaids, they **crash into the rocks**, causing them to sink.

If a mermaid falls in love with a human, she might choose to swap her tail for legs and live on land.

Mermaids and more

Mermaids are probably the most popular half-fish, half-human mythical beings, but **all sorts of merfolk** make the sea their home. There are stories across the world about **mermen** and **merchildren**, too.

Powerhouse predator

Lots of wildlife live in the jungles of **South America**, but they must watch out for one serious predator. For many centuries, stories have been shared of a giant snake that can swallow a **whole person** in a single bite!

Yacumama

Enter the jungle at your own risk! Legend has it that a **supersized serpent**, named Yacumama, lurks in rivers and swamps ready to eat the next person who passes by…

Water spirit

Yacumama is a staggering **30 m (100 ft) long** – about five times as long as a reticulated python, the longest snake in the world! She has blue skin and glowing eyes. Her name means "water mother", as she is believed to be the **protective water spirit** of the Amazon River. Catch her on a good day and she might bring heavy rains and schools of fish…

Ruthless hunter

… But catch Yacumama on a bad day and she can wreak havoc, causing **fierce storms**, **strong winds**, and **thick fog**. Her eyes hypnotize prey so that they freeze on the spot as she moves in for the kill. Fishers are her main target, as she likes to get her revenge on those who steal from her waters for their own profit.

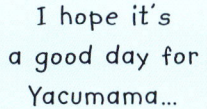

I hope it's a good day for Yacumama…

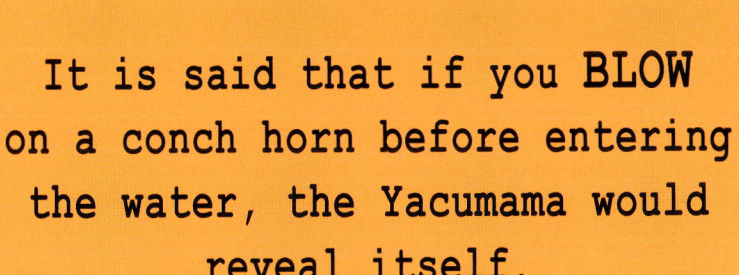

It is said that if you **BLOW** on a conch horn before entering the water, the Yacumama would reveal itself.

Few encounter Yacumama and live to tell the tale. One fisher got lucky during a trip in his canoe. As he cast his net, the shadow of Yacumama appeared. Fearing for his life, the fisher prayed – and his prayers were answered. Four tapirs dropped from the sky and made a splash in the water. With Yacumama distracted, the fisher was able to escape. But he vowed never to return.

Bunyip

This evil swamp monster is found in **First Nations Australian** folk stories. Nobody is sure what the Bunyip looks like – some say it is part human and part animal, while others think it looks like a fish or gorilla.

Water beast

The Bunyip lives in Australia's **wet places**, such as swamps, lagoons, water holes, and riverbeds. Being close to the **edge of the water** could be deadly, especially at night.

Bunyip beginnings

Once upon a time, the Bunyip was a person. When he didn't follow the rules set by the god, the Rainbow Snake, Bunyip was sent away to live on his own. Angry, Bunyip became an **evil spirit**.

Listen out!
I can be noisy, with
a terrifying HOWL.

Beware the Bunyip
Be careful, the Bunyip is extremely dangerous. He will kill and eat people that he comes across, especially women and children. He might try to lure you into the water, too.

Bunyip stories

The Bunyip doesn't just eat people – he can change them into other things, too. Here are two stories about Bunyip **transforming** people.

Swan surprise
One day, a man called Goondah was fishing for eels, but accidentally caught Bunyip's cub instead. In revenge, the Bunyip turned Goondah into a swan.

Branching together
A couple from the Frog tribe were separated by Bunyip. He turned them into two trees. As the trees grew, their branches reached out towards each other.

Ninki Nanka

If you come across the Ninki Nanka, look away! For it is said that one sighting of this dangerous, **dragon-like creature** proves fatal…

River beast

The people of **The Gambia** fear the Ninki Nanka, a river reptile that is said to be a mix between a **dragon** and a **serpent**. Its enormous body is the length of an Olympic swimming pool. Some say it has shiny scales, wings, and a feathery crest. Others say it has no limbs and slithers through the Gambia River.

Must-have mirror

According to legend, if you see the Ninki Nanka you will die. But, if the Ninki Nanka ever **sees itself**, it will also die. That's why explorers and fishers along the Gambia River carry a **mirror** with them.

Not all bad

In some stories, the Ninki Nanka changes from its monstrous form into a **rainbow** that fills the sky. It causes heavy rain, which fills the rivers and swamps with water and helps crops to thrive. So maybe Ninki Nanka isn't so bad after all!

Monster hunt

A team of experts went searching for the Ninki Nanka in 2006, thinking it was just a large monitor lizard. They spoke to a park ranger who claimed he saw the Ninki Nanka and only survived by swallowing a **magic potion**.

Visitors can travel 362 km (225 miles) up the Gambia River on a route called the NINKI NANKA TRAIL.

Mythical creatures

Beware the monsters that lurk in mythology and folklore. These creepy creatures are the stuff of nightmares, as blood-drinking vampires, screeching banshees, super-strong werewolves, and giant yetis emerge from their **shadowy underworlds**.

Ammit

Do you live a good life, without any wrongdoing? The **ancient Egyptians** believed that if you did not, your heart would be eaten by a demon called Ammit once you died.

Mixed-up monster

Ammit was a female demon. Her body was a strange mix of animals – she had the head of a **crocodile**, the front legs of a **lion**, and the back legs of a **hippopotamus**.

Ammit was a threat of what would

Welcome to the underworld

Ammit lived in the underworld. When ancient Egyptians died, they were sent to the underworld to have their **souls judged**. Only those who were thought to have behaved well in their lives would be allowed to stay there.

Weighing up

A person's heart was weighed against a feather on a pair of scales belonging to **Ma'at**, the goddess of truth and justice. If the heart was heavier than the feather, it was thrown to Ammit, who ate it.

Different names

Ammit is known by a number of names, many of which hint at her taste for **human flesh**. Here are some of them:

- Devourer of the Dead
- Demoness of Death
- Eater of Hearts
- Bone Eater

happen if you lived a SINFUL life.

Werewolves

These creepy fictional creatures are a mixture of the worst features of **humans** and **wolves**. Their bodies can change back and forth between human and wolf form.

Super strength

Werewolves are stronger than humans and wolves. They are also said to have **super senses**, such as a powerful sense of smell, which helps them hunt at night.

If a werewolf is WOUNDED as a wolf, the wounds

Stories about werewolves have been told in Europe for around a thousand years.

Many werewolves can't control whether or not they transform.

The full moon

Werewolves usually look like regular people. But once a month, when the Moon is full, **their bodies change** from human to wolf.

Becoming a werewolf

Legends say that a person becomes a werewolf if they are **cursed**, or if they are **bitten** or **scratched** by an existing werewolf. Earlier stories suggest that people could also change by covering themselves in a wolfskin.

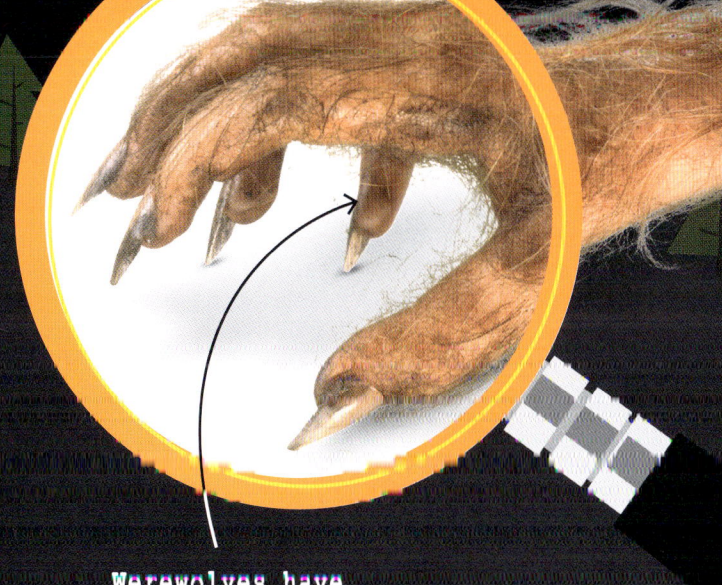

Werewolves have hairy, human-like hands with wolf-like claws.

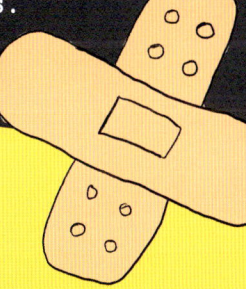

will show up on its HUMAN BODY, too.

Yetis

Yetis appear in legends from the **Himalayan Mountains** in Asia.

Yetis have another name, too: the Abominable (terrible) Snowman.

Is this the footprint of a Yeti or a big brown bear?

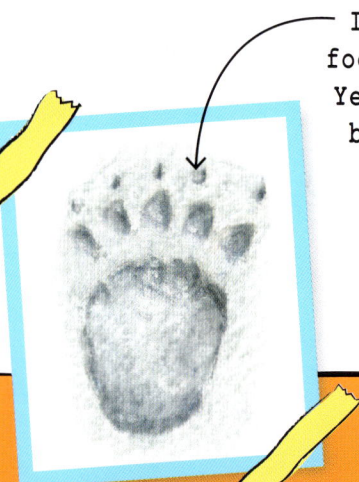

Yetis are covered in fur from head to foot.

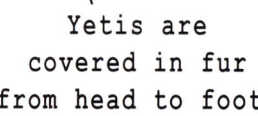

So far, there is NO SCIENTIFIC PROOF

Three Yetis

In **Tibet**, stories mention three different types of yetis:

1 The Nyalmo is huge. It is more than 2.5 m (8 ft) tall, is fierce, and has black fur.

2 The Chuti is medium-sized, up to 2 m (6.5 ft) tall.

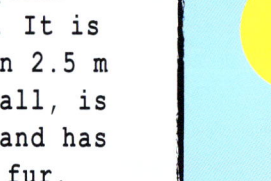
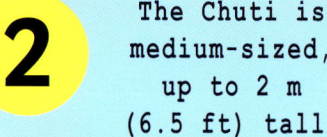

Yeti history

Tales of yetis have been told for centuries. They spread **around the world** in the 1950s when Tenzing Norgay and Sir Edmund Hillary climbed Mount Everest.

Hillary and Norgay claimed to see giant footprints on the slopes of the mountain.

Hardy beast

The Himalayas are **very cold**. The air is thin, and it is extremely windy. However, yetis have everything they need to live in such a barren place: thick fur, huge feet to stop them from sinking into the snow, and long, strong arms.

Bigfoot

On the other side of the world, in North America, there are stories about a similar ape-like creature called **Bigfoot**. Also known as Sasquatch, it is said to live in wild areas of the northwest USA.

that yetis exist. But they may just be very shy!

3

The Rang Shim Bombo is only around 1.5 m (5 ft) tall, with red-brown fur.

Brown bear

One Himalayan animal that could be confused with a yeti is the **brown bear**. It is large, can stand upright, and leaves big footprints.

Lumaluma

According to **First Nations Australian** legend, Lumaluma began as a huge whale, with an appetite to match!

Whale tale

Lumaluma was a wise whale who had learned sacred rituals. One day, he left the ocean and swam ashore in the **Northern Territory**, where he transformed into a giant human. Then, he began a journey inland.

Greedy giant

On his travels, Lumaluma told others about the sacred rituals he had learned. However, there was **delicious food** everywhere and he couldn't get enough of it. He often shared his rituals at great feasts and **ate all the food**.

A feast too far

Even when he wasn't invited, Lumaluma turned up and ate **everything**. When the food ran out, he scavenged for leftovers. Lumaluma finally went too far when he started trying to **eat the locals**! He had become too greedy for his own good.

Dead end

The **people grew angry** and decided enough was enough. Everyone gathered together and **attacked him**. Some stories say he survived and returned to the ocean in the form of a whale again…

Shared knowledge

Before he either died or went back to the ocean, Lumaluma gave the people all his knowledge. He told them about the special **Mardayin** ("sacred law") ceremony, including its ritual objects, ancestral songs, and symbolic markings to paint on themselves.

Vampires

Blood-drinking vampires appear in stories from all over the world. **European** vampires may look like humans, but they have special abilities that regular people can only dream of.

Vampire bat

Shape-shifting

Vampires can look very similar to humans, but they are able to **change** their appearance, which is called shape-shifting. They can transform into many things, including **bats**, **wolves**, or even a **cloud of mist**.

Long life

In Europe, vampires are seen as "**undead**" – their human lives are over, but they live on in vampire form. Some of them are hundreds, or even thousands, of years old.

The world's most famous vampire is Count Dracula. He appears in a book written by Bram Stoker, in 1897.

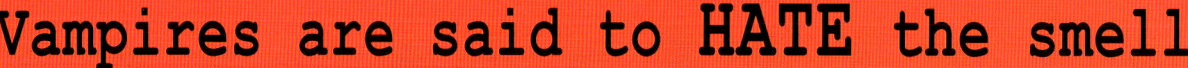

Vampires are said to HATE the smell

Undead bed

Sunlight burns pale vampire skin, so vampires only come out at night. In the day, vampires are said to sleep inside the **coffins** they were buried in.

Hard to kill

A vampire can only be destroyed by having its head cut off or a wooden post called a **stake** plunged into its heart.

Wooden stake

of garlic.

Garlic bulb

Bloodsuckers worldwide

Vampires aren't just found in Europe. Here are some examples of bloodsuckers from other parts of the **world**:

Peuchen

This huge, flying snake lives in South America. It hunts goats, which it can stop moving with just one glance.

Mandurugo

In the daytime, this Filipino vampire looks like a woman. At night, it becomes a flying monster with a spiky tongue.

Ramanga

This vampire from Madagascar eats nail clippings as well as drinking blood. It chooses powerful people as victims.

Chimera

This mythical monster's three fire-breathing heads struck fear into the hearts of the **ancient Greeks**.

Three in one

The Chimera had the head of a **lion**, the head of a **goat** on her back, and a **snake** for a tail. She had traits of these animals, too: a lion's strength, a goat's trickery, and a snake's venom.

The word Chimera means "SHE-GOAT" in Greek.

Fearsome family

The Chimera's parents were **Typhoeus**, a winged giant, and **Echidna**, half-woman, half-serpent. Her siblings included many-headed dogs Cerberus and Orthus, Hydra (a water monster), and Sphinx (a mix of human, lion, and bird).

Typhoeus

Echidna

Parents

Fire starter

The Chimera was found in **Lycia**, which was in what is now Turkey. She caused chaos, racing around and using her fiery breath to start fires and trigger **volcanoes**. When she started eating people, the ruler hatched a plan to put a stop to her wicked ways.

King Iobates of Lycia challenged the Greek hero Bellerophon to kill the Chimera. Bellerophon accepted, charging into battle on the winged horse Pegasus. He killed the Chimera and peace was restored to Lycia.

Cerberus

Orthus

Hydra

Sphinx

Siblings

Nian

A creature of **Chinese** folk tales, Nian was a fearsome beast who lived in the mountains. Each spring on the eve of Chinese Lunar New Year, it would come down looking for food and scaring the villagers.

> It's the evening before Lunar New Year – time for dinner!

The Chinese character "NIAN" means "NEW YEAR".

Beating the beast

In one tale, a wise old man came to a village on the night of Nian's visit. The villagers would usually flee to the mountains before nightfall to hide but the wise man knew the beast's **weaknesses**. So, he shared them with the terrified villagers.

1 **RED** Nian was afraid of the colour red, so the villagers put up bright red paper decorations.

2 **FIRE** Nian feared fire, so the people lit fires that burned all night to keep the monster away.

3 **NOISE** Nian was scared of loud noises, so the villagers set off firecrackers.

Nian looked like a lion.

Telling tales

Even though the legend of Nian dates back thousands of years, no record of the frightful beast exists in written folk tales. Like many other stories, the legend of Nian has been passed down through the generations by **word of mouth**.

Celebrating the New Year

Today, Chinese New Year is a **15-day festival**. To celebrate, families share special foods that bring luck and wealth. Children are given red gifts, including envelopes containing money.

Banshees

Beware the high-pitched cry of a wailing woman in **Irish** folklore. For it is said the sound of a banshee is a terrible omen of things to come…

wooooaaaaahh, woooooahhhh,

A cry in the dark

This **fairy-like spirit** is rarely seen, but often heard. When night falls, a banshee's ear-piercing **shriek** rings out in the darkness, bringing bad news to whoever is unfortunate enough to hear it.

According to legend,

Female forms

A banshee comes in different guises. She may be a **young woman** with long, flowing locks and red eyes from crying, an **older woman** with silver hair, or a wrinkly witch-like woman. These three versions reflect the characteristics of **Badhbh**, Celtic goddess of war and death.

Warning wail

A banshee supposedly moves close to a family and may haunt their home. When a family member is nearing the end of their life, the banshee produces a **loud screech** as though mourning them. This is her warning to the family that **death is coming**.

waaaaahhhhhhhhhh!

Origins of the story

Banshees are thought to be linked to the real life practice of keening, where women would traditionally sing **sad songs** at funerals and wakes.

Blast from the past

Some say a banshee is an **ancestor** that has come to warn their family of impending loss. Others believe she is the **restless spirit** of someone who died. Today, many people dismiss the banshee as an old-fashioned story.

SIX important irish families had their OWN banshees.

Bogeymen

Tales of bogeymen have frightened children for centuries. But parents usually only tell these scary stories to encourage **better behaviour**!

Tokoloshes

These small, **South African** bogeymen drink water to make themselves **invisible** and then play tricks on kids. It is believed that the only way to get rid of a tokoloshe is to call a witch doctor.

Cuca

Children in **Brazil** listen to a horrible lullaby. The words warn them that if they are still awake after bedtime, they can expect a visit from Cuca, an old, hungry, **crocodile woman**. So turn off the lights and go to sleep if you want to avoid her.

Namahage

On New Year's Eve in **Japan**, demons wearing **ogre masks** stomp around looking for naughty children. The Namahage take the rude and lazy children away.

Wewe Gombel

Indonesia's bogeyman is different. Wewe Gombel wants to help children who have **bad or lazy parents** and look after them herself in her treetop nest. If the parents want their children back, they must promise to change their ways. Don't forget to tell your grownups this one!

These bogeyman stories might seem scary, but don't believe everything you hear!

El Hombre Del Saco

Meaning "**sack man**", El Hombre Del Saco is found in **Spain**. This old man is said to take children who are walking alone and carry them off in his sack. If he's hungry, he eats them, and if he's full up, he sells them – so, it's probably better not to wander off in the first place!

Butzemanns

In **Germany**, a **ghostly goblin** in a cloak is said to hide under the bed or inside the wardrobe. He hangs around waiting to pop out if children misbehave at bedtime.

69

Strange beginnings

For a basilisk to be born, the egg must be laid by a **cockerel** – not a hen. This must happen in a nest made of toad dung, and the egg should be hatched out by a snake or toad.

Basilisks

Basilisks are very strange looking creatures. They have the wings, crest, and claws of a **rooster**, but the body of a **dragon-like reptile**.

Basilisks are also known

Death stare

Basilisks are extremely dangerous. They can kill plants and animals with a single glance from their **shining eyes**. Never look a basilisk in the eye! They are sometimes said to turn their victims into lumps of solid stone. They can also kill by **hissing**.

as COCKATRICES.

Devil lizard
In stories from **medieval Europe**, a basilisk was often used as a stand-in for the devil. It was linked with disease and sickness.

The name "basilisk" is ancient Greek for "little king".

Enemies of a basilisk

Basilisks are almost impossible to kill. There are just two animals that can manage it: **weasels** and **cockerels**. Weasels produce a venom deadly to basilisks. Cockerels can kill a basilisk just by crowing.

Cock-a-doodle-do!

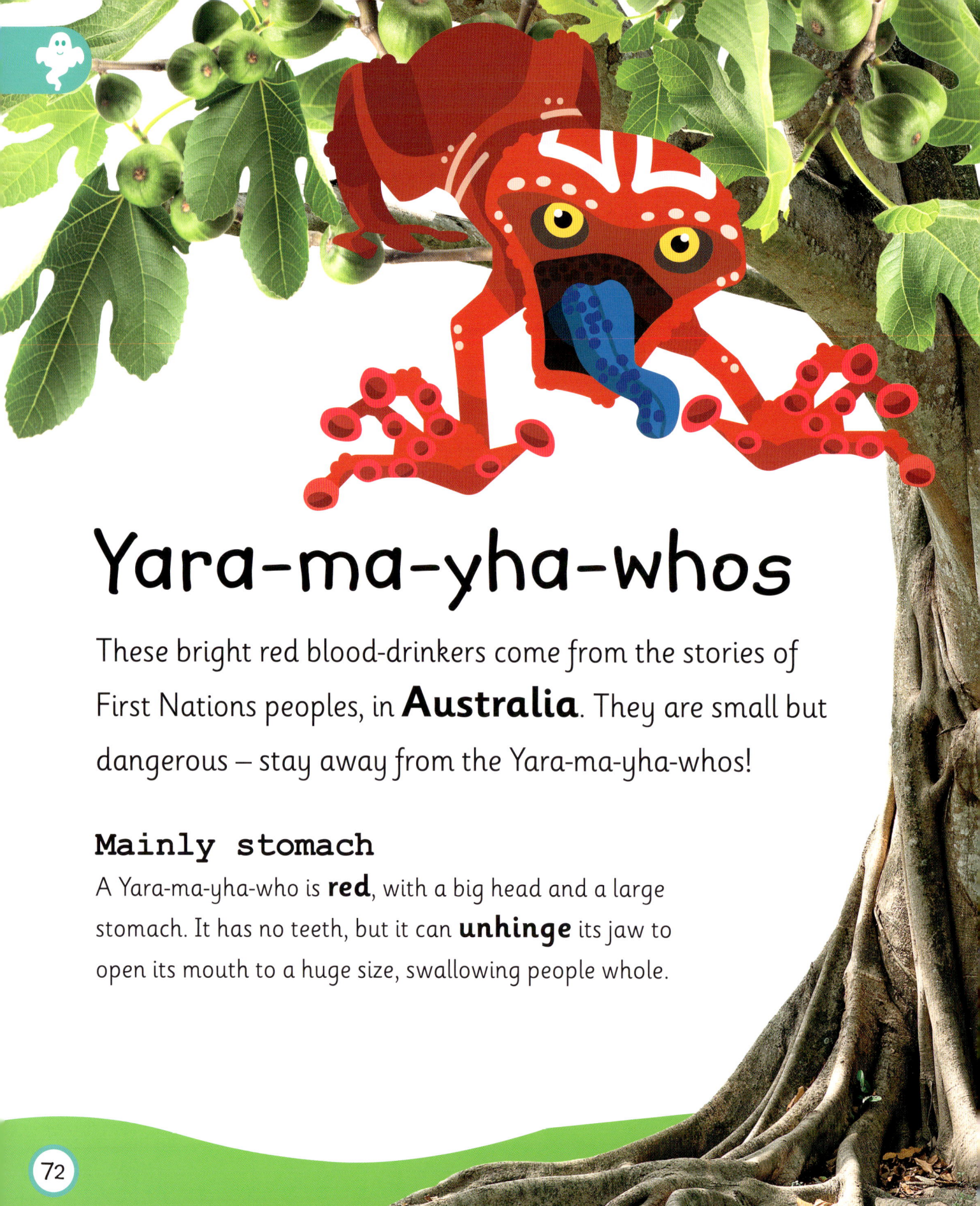

Yara-ma-yha-whos

These bright red blood-drinkers come from the stories of First Nations peoples, in **Australia**. They are small but dangerous – stay away from the Yara-ma-yha-whos!

Mainly stomach

A Yara-ma-yha-who is **red**, with a big head and a large stomach. It has no teeth, but it can **unhinge** its jaw to open its mouth to a huge size, swallowing people whole.

Fig tree

Patient beast

To catch a victim, a Yara-ma-yha-who **sits quietly**, high in the branches of a fig tree. Fig trees have thick layers of leaves, so the creature is well-hidden. When someone walks below, the Yara-ma-yha-who **drops down** on them from above.

Hard work

A Yara-ma-yha-who uses **suction cups** on its fingers and toes to suck the blood of its victims. It then swallows them whole, before vomiting them out again.

Transformation

Each time a person is **swallowed** by a Yara-ma-yha-who they will become a **little bit smaller**. If they are swallowed over again enough times, they will eventually become a Yara-ma-yha-who themselves.

Though scary, a Yara-ma-yha-who can easily be outrun, because it is very SLOW.

Qilins

These **Chinese** creatures are thought to bring **peace** and **prosperity** to anyone who catches a glimpse.

Rare but rich

A qilin is a beast with four **hooves**, a **mane** on its back, a **scaly body**, and **horns** on its head. A rare sighting of a qilin brings only serenity, success, and wealth.

Gentle by nature

Unlike many mythical beasts, a qilin is **peaceful and gentle**. It is said to walk on clouds because it doesn't want to hurt the grass by stepping on it. It also avoids eating plants in case they feel any pain.

The qilin dance is performed at the CHINESE LUNAR NEW YEAR in honour of these much-loved creatures.

Chinese mythology suggests you may see a qilin at the start or end of a worthy ruler's reign or at the birth or death of a wise person. It is said that a qilin appeared at the birth of the Chinese philosopher Confucius as a positive omen of what he would go on to become.

Feeling the heat

A qilin grows more powerful in the presence of evil so that it can protect the vulnerable and innocent. **Sizzling flames** burst from its mouth to show that the qilin is not to be messed with. Today you can spot a qilin as one of the **honorary statues** that guard Chinese palaces and temples.

Qilin statue at the Summer Palace in Beijing, China

Medusa

On an island far away live Medusa and her sisters – human-like monsters with snakes instead of hair. Their story is told as part of **ancient Greek** legend.

The Gorgons

Medusa had two sisters, **Stheno** and **Euryale**. They were known as the **Gorgons**. They had scaly skin and hair made of snakes.

Medusa was the only Gorgon who could be killed – her sisters were immortal.

Special sister

Unlike her sisters, Medusa had a unique ability – she could **turn people to stone** with just one look. The sisters lived on an island, which was covered in statues that were once people.

Stheno

Medusa was killed by the Greek hero Perseus. He approached her by only looking at her reflection in his shiny, mirror-like shield. Once close enough, he drew his sword and cut off her head.

Perseus putting Medusa's head in a sack.

Medusa

Stony powers

Medusa's head could turn people to stone even after she died. Perseus kept it in a sack and used it as a **weapon**, to turn his enemies to stone.

Euryale

Ghosts

Throughout history , there have been many spooky stories about dead spirits that walk the Earth and **visit the living**. But ghosts aren't all scary – they range from friendly floaty figures to trick-playing poltergeists. Enter this ghostly gallery to find out more…

Many people believe that ghosts are the

Haunted houses

Many ghost stories revolve around a specific place. Some spirits may return to haunt the house where they lived or the **place where they died**. The ghost of Anne Boleyn, one of King Henry VIII's wives, is rumoured to haunt the home where she grew up.

Poltergeists

Meaning "**noisy spirit**" in German, poltergeists really live up to their name! Although these playful spirits cannot be seen, they can certainly be heard slamming doors and making loud banging sounds. They love to send **objects flying** suddenly across the room.

SLAM!

Say cheese

The invention of the camera gave ghost hunters the chance to take **photographs of ghosts** Shadowy figures, blurred bodies, and cloaked phantoms have all shown up on film. But, many people think these photos of ghosts are just tricks of the light, water droplets on the lens, or deliberate fakes.

A ghost or a hoax?

SOULS of people who have died.

Day of the Dead

Mexican people celebrate the Day of the Dead festival at the beginning of November. This is an important occasion to **remember family and friends** who have died. It's thought that their souls or ghosts visit Earth again.

Daimonji

This Japanese festival, held on 16 August, marks the end of Obon. This is when family members who have died come back to Earth for a few days. Huge bonfires and lanterns are lit to **send the ghosts off** to the spirit world again.

Flying high

People have kept their eyes on the skies since ancient times, telling stories of winged horses, colossal birds, and dragons. These creatures bring **warnings** of things to come, **messages** from the gods, or simply symbolize the incredible **power of nature**. Time to join some aerial adventures…

Griffins

Strong, fierce griffins are thought of as guardians of all that is good, and protectors against all that is evil. Legends about griffins are told across **three continents**: Europe, Asia, and Africa.

Guarding gold

Griffins stand guard over piles of treasure – their favourite being **gold**. Some say that griffins lay eggs full of gold, and others say that they build their nests from solid gold.

Lion

Eagle

Lion and eagle

A griffin has the head and wings of an **eagle**, with the body and tail of a **lion**. Some griffins also have eagle claws on their front feet.

Healing powers

Some griffin body parts have **magical powers**. A touch of a griffin's feather is said to have the power to return sight to someone who is blind. A griffin's claw is also able to cure all sorts of diseases.

Eagle feather

Noble bird

A griffin can be a symbol of **royalty**. It appears on many different shields and coats of arms. Having a griffin on your shield showed that the family you worked for were rich and powerful.

Hippogriff

The child of a male griffin and a female horse is called a hippogriff. A hippogriff has the head and wings of an **eagle** and the body and legs of a **horse**.

Pegasus

Most horses are stuck on the ground, but Pegasus had wings that let him fly. He was also immortal. The story of Pegasus comes from **ancient Greece**.

Pegasus could

Born from death

Pegasus's birth was very unusual. His mother was **Medusa**. When the hero Perseus cut off Medusa's head, Pegasus was born from the wound.

Medusa

Bellerophon used a magical rein to tame Pegasus.

Bellerophon

The Greek hero Bellerophon tamed Pegasus and the pair flew around, **destroying monsters**. One day, Bellerophon decided to ride Pegasus up to join the gods. This made Zeus, King of the gods, angry and he caused Bellerophon to fall off Pegasus and die.

After Bellerophon died, Pegasus went to live with the gods. He became the servant of Zeus. Pegasus's jobs for Zeus included carrying magical lightning bolts and pulling his chariot.

create a stream by STAMPING ON THE GROUND with his hoof.

Starry memory

To thank Pegasus for his long service, Zeus turned him into stars and sprinkled them across the night sky. These stars form the **constellation** Pegasus, which can be seen in our skies today.

Pegasus constellation

Thunderbird appears in many songs, stories, and artworks.

Thunderbird

Flying through the folklore of **North America** is Thunderbird. It appears in the stories of many Indigenous peoples, sometimes as a bird or spirit, and sometimes in human form.

Ancient bird

The story of Thunderbird may be based on **Aiolornis**, a type of bird that would have been living in North America when the first humans arrived. Aiolornis were large and fed on dead whales.

Wild weather

Thunderbird is connected with the weather. It creates **storms** as it flies through the air – its flapping wings stir up winds and rain clouds. Thunderbird's wings are also said to make the sound of **rolling thunder**.

Incredible bird

As birds go, Thunderbird is **absolutely huge**. It has a curved beak that ends in a sharp point, glowing eyes, and colossal claws. Thunderbird is strong and powerful, as well as magical and wise.

Thunderbird at the top of the totem pole.

Position of power

Thunderbird is often shown at the very tops of **totem poles** – carved and painted tree trunks crafted by some Indigenous peoples. Its high position shows how important it is.

Food for all

In one Thunderbird myth, the Quileute people couldn't find any food. Desperate, they prayed to the **Great Spirit** for help. The next day, Thunderbird appeared carrying a **huge whale**, which it gave to the hungry people to eat.

Thunderbird is sometimes said to PUNISH people who break rules.

Big Owl

The **Apache** people in North America feared Big Owl, a giant bird of prey that lived up to its name. You didn't want to see this bird — especially when it was hungry!

Scary sight

Standing taller than an adult man, Big Owl **dominated** the night skies. It had snow-white feathers, huge eyes, powerful wings, and sharp talons.

Feathered friends

This fearsome creature may be based on real life. Southwest USA and Mexico are home to **big birds**, so it is possible that a genuine sighting of a giant owl brought about the story.

Knot

Shape-shifting witch

There are other owls in mythology, such as **La Lechuza**. La Lechuza was once a woman who sold her soul to the devil to get magical powers and **become a witch**. By day, she was a witch, but by night she shape-shifted into a large owl to take revenge on the world.

After dark

Big Owl would spot a target from the air and fly low in the darkness. From adults to small children, **no one was safe** if Big Owl was hungry. It would grab its victim and fly home to eat its dinner.

Legend goes that WHISTLING three times at midnight would bring Big Owl to your door.

Safety first

Traditional weapons didn't work against Big Owl. Instead, tying seven **knots** in a rope by the front door and rubbing **salt** around windows at night stopped it coming close.

salt

Heavy dinner

A roc needed to eat large amounts to satisfy its hunger. It would carry off **animals** including horses, cows, and even elephants! Some accounts describe a roc as being able to pick up **whole ships** full of people.

For many years, people believed that rocs were REAL.

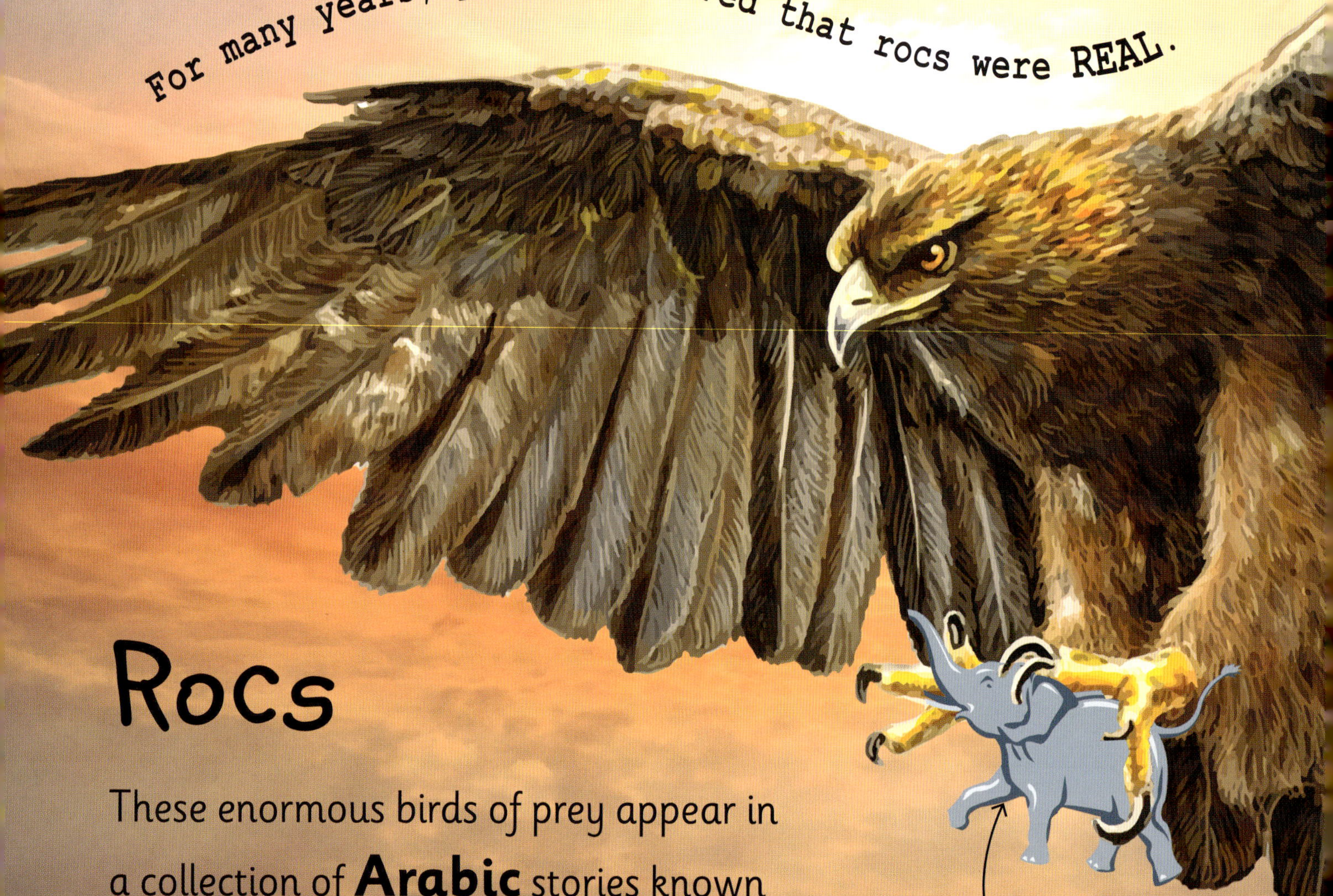

Rocs

These enormous birds of prey appear in a collection of **Arabic** stories known as One Thousand and One Nights. Some stories describe rocs as being so big that they can block the Sun if they fly in front of it.

Rocs could carry large animals such as elephants.

Unlucky sighting

Seeing a roc was very **unlucky**. Spotting one could mean that either your **crops** would fail and die, or that there would soon be a battle, with many **deaths**.

Italian explorer Marco Polo claimed to have seen a roc in Madagascar, an island off the eastern coast of Africa.

Hitchhiking on a roc

Sinbad was stuck on an island. He came across a huge egg and went to take a closer look. Then, an enormous roc landed next to the egg. It didn't notice him, and he used his turban to tie himself to one of the roc's legs. When the roc flew away, it took Sinbad with him.

A big mistake

Sinbad and his crew cooked a huge roc egg they found on a beach, and then they gathered onto their ship to escape. When the two roc parents of the egg returned, they were really angry. They pelted the sailors and their ship with boulders. All the sailors except Sinbad were killed.

Sinbad the sailor

Two of the **One Thousand and One Nights stories** feature rocs, as well as a sailor called Sinbad.

91

Phoenixes

Phoenixes are firebirds that live for hundreds of years. They are immortal — they never die completely, but loop through an **endless cycle** of death and rebirth.

A fiery end

At the end of its life, a tired phoenix builds a nest from myrrh, a sweet-scented tree resin. Then the nest **catches fire** with the phoenix sitting in it.

DEATH

A phoenix lives for around 500 YEARS.

Phoenix nest catching fire

Myrrh twigs

Myrrh tree

It is impossible to tell a LIE

1

Some legends say that ONLY ONE phoenix exists at a time.

The lifecycle of a phoenix

Born again

Several days after its death, the very same phoenix **hatches** from an egg in the ashes of its nest. The phoenix begins living all over again.

REBIRTH

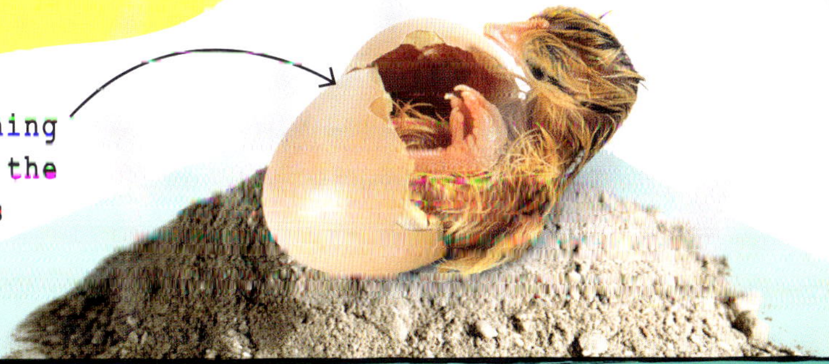

Hatching from the ashes

if a phoenix is nearby.

Ancient inspiration

The phoenix first appears in ancient Greek legends from thousands of years ago. It may have been inspired by stories from ancient Egypt. They feature a bird god called **Bennu**, who was a symbol of rebirth.

The bird god Bennu

A phoenix is seen as a symbol of hope and good luck.

Honestly, I'm telling the TRUTH!

Unicorns

The unicorn is a pure white, horse-like creature with a single spiral horn on its head. Stories about it have been told across **Europe** and **Asia** for thousands of years.

The unicorn is the national animal of Scotland, UK.

Noble animal

Unicorns are **peaceful** creatures that cannot harm people in any way. They are unable to do bad things at all – unicorns can only do **good**.

Unicorn eyes are blue or purple.

A unicorn horn is called an "ALICORN".

The narwhal is a type of whale that lives in Arctic waters. It has a long, spiral tusk that has often been mistaken for a unicorn horn. This confusion meant that narwhal horns were once worth 20 times their weight in gold.

Magical horn

A unicorn's beautiful spiral horn has **magic powers**. Here are a few of them:

1 If a unicorn's horn is dipped into water, the water will become **pure** and safe to drink.

2 A cup made from a unicorn horn **stops poison** from working.

3 A unicorn horn can **stop sickness**, and make people well again.

Hard to catch

Just because unicorns don't hurt people, it doesn't mean that humans don't try to **hurt them** in stories. However, they are extremely fast and clever, making them very hard to catch.

Garuda

In **Hindu** mythology, Garuda was king of all birds. This huge half-human, half-bird hybrid was determined to destroy any evil in its path.

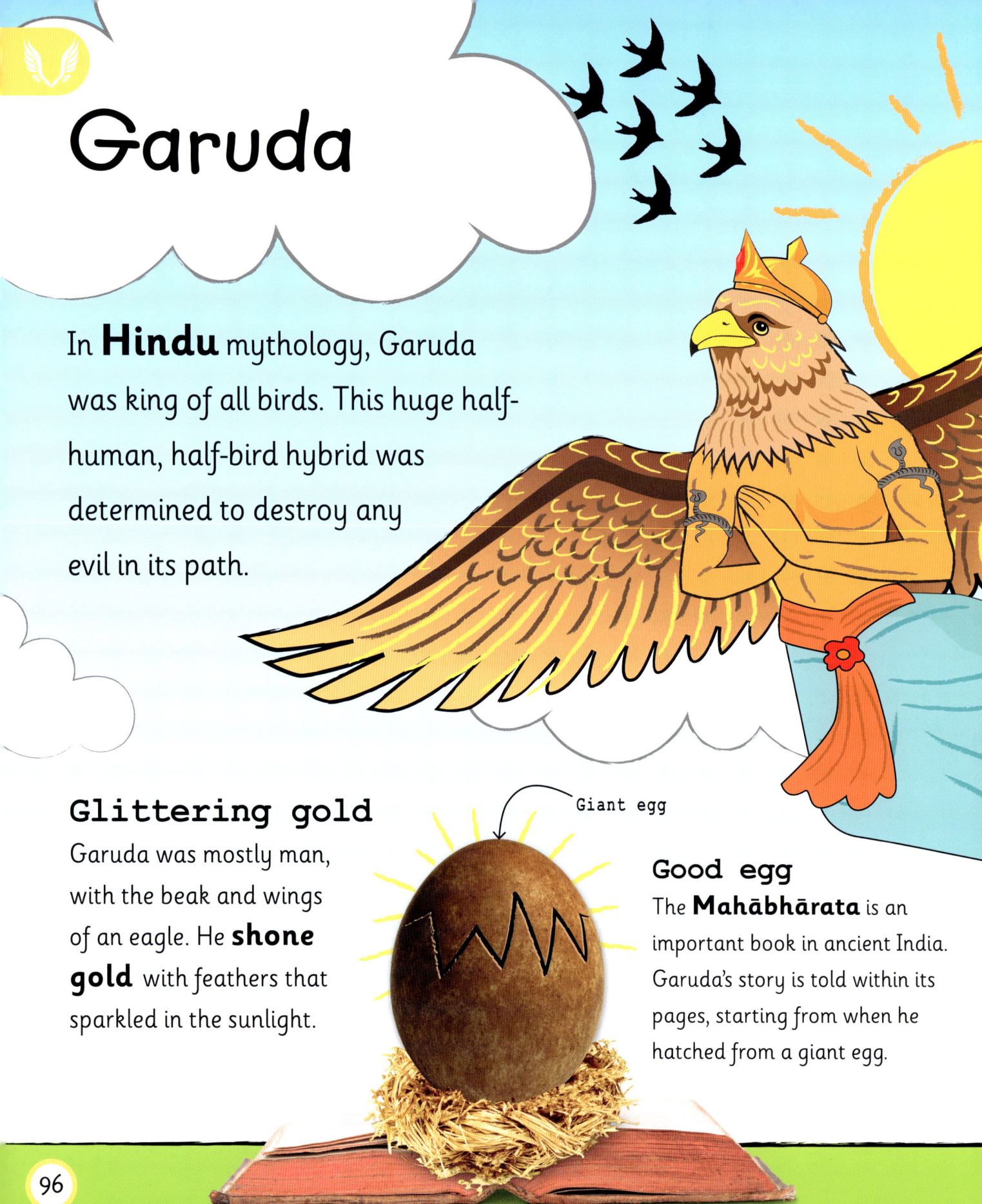

Glittering gold

Garuda was mostly man, with the beak and wings of an eagle. He **shone gold** with feathers that sparkled in the sunlight.

Giant egg

Good egg

The **Mahābhārata** is an important book in ancient India. Garuda's story is told within its pages, starting from when he hatched from a giant egg.

Up, up, and away!

The Hindu god of preservation, **Vishnu**, rode on the back of Garuda. Together they flew across the skies.

Vishnu riding on the back of Garuda

Dark deed

Garuda hated the **nagas**. They were half-human, half-snake and imprisoned his mother in the underworld.

Nagas had the face of a man and a snake-like lower body.

Garuda fighting the nagas

Snake slayer

Garuda wanted vengeance for his mother and, with Vishnu on his back, he fought the nagas for **all eternity**.

Dragons

Chinese dragon

These mythical beasts take **different forms** in various cultures. Chinese dragons are serpent-shaped bringers of luck. In Europe, they are winged, fire-breathing monsters.

The komodo dragon is the world's BIGGEST LIZARD and the

Mesopotamian myth

The terrifying ancient Mesopotamian dragon **Tiamat** was fought by **Marduk**. One half became heaven and the other became Earth.

Drawing of Tiamat

Dragon's den

Ljubljana, Slovenia, is known as the "city of dragons". A dragon is on the city's coat of arms and is the **guardian** who **protects** the city.

Statue at Dragon Bridge, Ljubljana, Slovenia

Fáfnir the dragon

Norse dragon

In one Norse story, a dragon named **Fáfnir** stood guard over a mountain of treasure. He was slain by **Sigurd**, the son of a king, who wanted the treasure for himself. Sigurd bathed in Fáfnir's blood to make himself unbeatable in future.

Komodo dragons live on islands in Indonesia.

closest thing to a **MYTHICAL DRAGON**.

Water dragon

Kuzuryū is a Japanese dragon that lives in water. It once brought bad luck, until a priest blessed it and turned it into a nine-headed **protector** dragon.

Bronze statue of Kuzuryū, Hakone, Japan

Grotesque Gargouille

In medieval France, the **Gargouille** appeared from the river and flooded the land, before a bishop stopped it. Today, gargoyles protect buildings.

Gargoyle statue, Paris, France

Harpies

In **ancient Greek** mythology, a harpy had the **head of a woman** and the **body of a bird**. They were greedy robbers sent by the gods to punish people on Earth.

Harpy

Harpy hybrid

Harpies were huge, with sharp talons. Their name means "**snatcher**". They were once winged spirits that controlled the wind and rain, but over time, they grew more terrifying and became **servants** of the gods.

Hounds of Zeus

Chief god Zeus sent the harpies to **punish wrongdoers** on Earth, so they became known as the "hounds of Zeus". The worst punishment was when the harpies sunk their **talons into a victim** and carried them off to the underworld forever.

Zeus

Royal rebel

Phineus, a Greek king, had the ability to see into the future. He revealed **secrets** about the gods' plans. Furious, the gods sent harpies to **punish him**. Whenever he tried to eat, the harpies would fly down and steal his food. The king began to starve and was saved by the Argonauts, led by hero Jason, who scared off the harpies.

King Phineus

Angry harpies

Pretty as a picture

Harpies weren't always shown as hideous creatures in ancient Greek **art and literature**. The poet Homer described a beautiful harpy called Podarge in his epic poem *The Odyssey*. Light-footed Podarge controlled the wind and guided ships to safety.

Harpy on a vase

The harpy eagle of Central and South America is named after the harpies in Greek mythology.

Amaterasu

The **Japanese** Sun goddess plunged the world into **darkness**, but soon returned to shine her light forever more...

Celestial shine

Amaterasu was the daughter of creator god Izanagi, and became the **Sun goddess**. On Earth, she shone so brightly that she **burned the ground**, so she flew into the sky to look after the heavens instead.

Tsukuyomi

Family ties

Amaterasu's siblings were Moon god **Tsukuyomi**, who looked after the night sky, and storm god **Susanoo**, who controlled the seas. Today, it is said the Japanese royal family descend from Amaterasu and family.

Susanoo

Left in the dark

Susanoo wanted to reign over the underworld rather than the seas. But he didn't get his way, so he decided to cause trouble. He threw a dead horse at Amaterasu, and she decided enough was enough! She **hid in a cave** in protest, and the world turned dark without her sunlight.

Dancing in the moonlight

The gods and goddesses placed crowing cockerels and glittering jewels at the entrance of Amaterasu's cave, but she didn't come out. It was only when the goddess of merry-making, **Uzume**, did a **funny dance** that she came out to see what was making everyone laugh.

Uzume

Sun shrine

When Amaterasu left the cave, the **world lit up**! The crops could grow, and the gods and goddesses were happy. They blocked the entrance to the cave so that Amaterasu could never hide there again.

The Grand Shrine of Ise in Japan honours Amaterasu.

Home in the sky

Ukko lived in the very centre of the sky, in heaven. Because of this, he was also known as **Jumala** – "Heaven God". Ukko was thought of as the **chief** of all the Finnish gods.

Ukko

The great Ukko is the god of sky and thunder in folk religion from **Finland**. He ruled over the gods from his position high in the sky.

Protecting warriors

Warriors **prayed** to Ukko for protection, because he was so powerful. They hoped he would give them **magic charms**, which would keep them safe in battles.

Ukko's wedges

Wedge-shaped stones are linked to Ukko. They were worn on necklaces, and were thought to keep people safe from evil spirits and fire.

Weather god

As god of the sky, Ukko could **control the weather**. He used thunderbolts as weapons, and had an axe or hammer that could produce jets of lightning. He travelled through the sky on a chariot, which made the sound of thunder.

New life

Ukko controlled how much **rain** fell, so he could also control how well **plants grew**. People made sacrifices to him when they planted crops or when there wasn't enough water. They also asked for his help when babies and calves were being born.

105

Magic and mischief

Cultures around the world have told tales of magic and mischief, featuring characters who **unleash chaos** using their clever cunning, magical powers, or shape-shifting abilities. However, these troublesome folk should not just be taken at face value. Their magic and trickery may cause mayhem, but they teach **important life lessons**.

Anansi

For centuries, the **Ashanti** people of West Africa have shared stories about the trickster spider, Anansi. Weaving a web of trouble, he has taught generations of children important life lessons.

Anansi's powers

Anansi started out in human form, but took the form of a spider. There are many stories about Anansi. Some say that his **powers** were so strong that he created the Sun and the Moon and controlled the rain and the oceans.

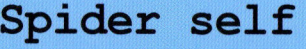

Total trickster

Anansi was known for playing tricks, including on other animals. Some stories say that the sky god, **Nyame**, punished Anansi by turning him into a spider.

Spider self

Anansi became **part spider**, part human. He was mostly a spider, but could also take human form. Despite his transformation, Anansi still got up to his old tricks.

A dangerous challenge

Nyame was said to own all the stories in the world. Nyame said Anansi could only have them if he captured four of the most **dangerous creatures** – a python, a jaguar, hornets, and a fairy.

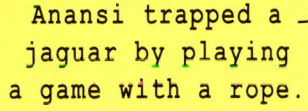

Anansi trapped a jaguar by playing a game with a rope.

He tricked hornets by offering them a box to escape the rain.

Knowledge is power

Anansi used cunning to trap animals, such as tricking hornets by offering them shelter. Nyame was so impressed that he gave Anansi a collection of stories, known as the **wisdom narratives**.

Spoken stories

These stories of Anansi started in Ghana during the 1500s and were told at bedtime in African villages. Children learned of Anansi and **word soon spread**. They are known today as "spider stories".

Did you know?
Legend goes that when he won the wisdom narratives, Anansi collected all the world's wisdom for himself. But when it started spilling over, he decided to share his knowledge with everyone.

Maui

Maui was a mischief-making, heroic demigod. He used his trickster talents to outwit gods and help humankind. His stories centre around **Polynesia**, a vast area of the Pacific Ocean from New Zealand to Hawaii.

Maui

Fishing for islands

Maui had a curved, magic fish hook. One day, when he cast the hook out into the sea, he felt a tug on its line. Pulling with all his might, he dragged a piece of land from the ocean to the surface. This was the first of the **Polynesian islands** for humans to live on.

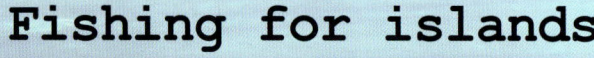

Fish hook

Maui could SHAPE-SHIFT into different

Raising the sky

Legends say the sky above the Polynesian islands was made of solid **blue stone** and lay so close to the ground that people could barely stand. Maui used his strength to push the sky away from the ground, giving the people more space.

Maui lifting the Polynesian sky

Snaring the Sun

Ra, the Sun, used to move through the sky so quickly that people had little time in the light to do their work. So Maui devised a plan. He set up ropes to **trap** Ra as he rose. Ra apologized and promised to move more slowly, so the days grew longer.

Cheating death

Maui wanted eternal life for himself and humankind. So he shape-shifted into a lizard and crawled into the body of **Hine-nui-te-pō**, the goddess of death, while she slept. When she woke up however, she crushed Maui and made sure humans couldn't live forever.

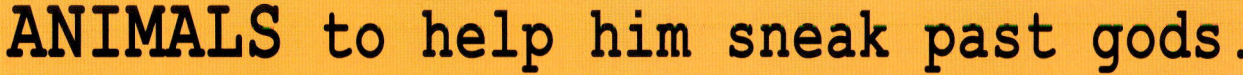
ANIMALS to help him sneak past gods.

Saci-pererê

Now you see him – now you don't! Saci-pererê is a **Brazilian** mischief-maker best known for his disappearing act.

A magical red cap gives Saci special powers.

Trickster traveller

Saci-pererê is a man with one leg, a pipe, and a magical red cap. He travels around on a **hurricane**, making him tricky to catch!

Saci travels on a magical hurricane.

Prized possession

Saci's magical red cap allows him to **disappear** and **reappear**. If you take his cap, he will make any wish come true – as long as he gets his hat back!

Brazil celebrates Saci-pererê's NATIONAL DAY

Up to his old tricks

Saci is usually up to **no good**. He makes a mess in the kitchen, hides toys, tangles sewing, leaves nails lying around, and more!

Saci spills and burns food.

He leaves sharp nails on the ground.

Blame game

When things go wrong, families blame Saci. Even when someone loses their **own belongings**, they still say he is the culprit. Saci is also said to cause hurricane-force winds.

Saci scares farm animals and makes dogs bark.

every year on 31 OCTOBER.

Great escape

If Saci is troubling someone, they have **three** options:

1 **Cross a stream**. Saci won't travel across water because he loses his magical powers.

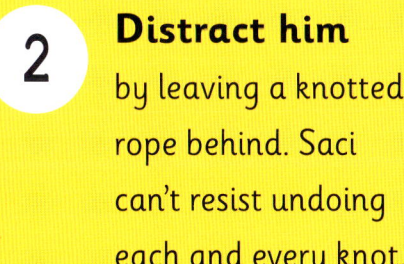

2 **Distract him** by leaving a knotted rope behind. Saci can't resist undoing each and every knot.

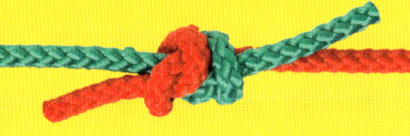

3 **Offer him tobacco** for his pipe to get on his good side.

Rainbow Snake

At the heart of the **Australian First Nations** culture is the Rainbow Snake. This creator god brings new life, and helps plants and animals to grow.

First Nations cave painting of the "Rainbow Snake"

Remarkable reptile

This snake made and **shaped Earth**. It was at least 6 m (20 ft) long — the same as three bathtubs.

Rainbow maker

The Rainbow Snake was said to live under **water holes** in the desert. A **rainbow** showed where it was moving between water holes.

Rainbow Snakes have been found on

Rise and fall

The snake would bring **rain** to keep nature alive. Sometimes it would bring too much or too little rain, to punish bad behaviour.

Australian waterhole

Nature's way

The legend of the Rainbow Snake teaches people to **respect nature** and the land they live on.

Dreamtime

In First Nations culture, the Dreamtime was the beginning of the world, when Rainbow Snake awoke and **created everything**.

First Nations people performing rituals

First Nations ritual

First Nations people still **show their respect** to the Rainbow Snake. They follow a special ritual before drinking at water holes.

First Nations ROCK ART from more than 6,000 YEARS ago.

Snake painted on a boomerang

Coyote

The **Indigenous peoples** of **North America** tell tales of Coyote, a cunning canine that existed on Earth before humans, and caused mayhem!

Magical coyote

Although Coyote usually took the form of a large, **wolf-like dog**, he could also **shape-shift** into a human or disappear altogether. He was a curious trickster who often landed in trouble, but was sometimes the hero, too.

Saving the day

Coyote features in many creator stories. In one story, a monster began eating all of Earth's animals, so Coyote let himself be **swallowed**, too. Then, from inside its tummy, Coyote killed the monster and saved the animals.

Some communities still perform a traditional COYOTE

Comic character

In other more humorous stories, Coyote is a useless hunter who **copies other animals** with bad results. He once jumped off a cliff expecting to soar like an eagle, but he fell to the ground and his brother had to put him back together again!

Creating chaos

Some communities see Coyote as a problem. He has been described as **throwing up stars** and leaving them scattered in a mess. Another tale tells of Coyote stealing the babies of Water Buffalo, who gets revenge by unleashing an almighty flood. These tales warn people not to be selfish like Coyote.

Survival experts

Coyotes now live all over North America, and their populations may be many millions. Unlike the Coyote in legends, these coyotes are successful hunters and can attack **deer** and **elk**. If needed, they can survive on small prey such as insects and mice, or **scavenge** for leftovers.

DANCE in honour of Coyote.

Mischievous creatures

Watch out for these naughty little folk! Tales of mischievous creatures are told around the world. Their names may change, but their **trickery** stays the same.

Sprites

These tiny, winged creatures live deep in the woods. Sprites make low-level mischief such as **hiding belongings**, **knocking things over**, or **chasing butterflies**. They fly in groups, zipping around to surprise the wildlife.

Leprechauns

In **Irish** folklore, these tiny old men are masters of meddling. They make shoes during the day, but turn naughty at night, **playing tricks** and **having parties** until dawn. Leprechauns look after a crock of gold, but they vanish with their stash if anyone tries to take it!

Pixies

Found in **British**, **German**, and **Scandinavian** folklore, pixies look like small children and wear hats and old clothes. They are kind, but when they get bored, they **bang on walls** and **blow out candles**!

Elves

These magical creatures are from **German**, **Norse**, and **Celtic** folklore and can be naughty or nice. The most famous elves are **Santa's helpers**, but German elves are pranksters who cause **bad dreams**.

Imps

These little demon-like creatures originate in **German** folklore. They are usually **fun-loving**, **cheeky**, and **naughty**, rather than evil. Often, they are found **playing tricks** on humans. In some stories, they are the servants of witches and wizards.

Brownies

In **Scottish** folklore, these hardworking characters live in houses and come out at night to **clean** and **do chores**. However, they expect a delicious bowl of milk or porridge in return, and there will be **trouble** if they don't get it!

Dokkaebi

Korean people have told stories about dokkaebi for many years. Dokkaebi are goblin-like **nature spirits**. Some are helpful but others like to annoy people.

Dokkaebi looks

There are lots of different types of dokkaebi. Generally they have human-like bodies, with **red faces**, **sharp horns**, and **bulging eyes**. They are also quite hairy.

Most dokkaebi are completely HARMLESS.

Many skills

Dokkaebi have **magic powers**, **super strength**, and are able to **fly**. They are also said to like wrestling and playing tricks on people.

Long, bell-shaped skirt

Jeogori

Well-dressed

Some dokkaebi wear **hanbok** – **traditional Korean clothing**. The top part is called a jeogori. Women wear the jeogori with a long, bell-shaped skirt. Men wear it with baggy trousers.

Tricking a dokkaebi

It is hard to trick a dokkaebi because they are very **clever**. However, one person is said to have managed it:

A farmer asked a dokkaebi what it was afraid of, and it said blood. When the dokkaebi asked what the farmer was afraid of, he said money.

The farmer then spread blood around his house, making the dokkaebi angry.

As revenge, the dokkaebi threw bags of money at the farmer, not realising this made the farmer rich and happy.

Lazy bones

Hare features in many African trickster stories. He is extremely **confident** and believes that he is better than all the other animals. While he has many clever ideas, Hare has a history of **laziness** and this tends to be **his downfall**.

ZZ

Hare

This quick and cunning **African trickster** always outwits other animals, but even he can be **outsmarted**!

Preparing to plant

In one story, the animals needed to plant crops. Hare didn't want to work, so he suggested that a **hippopotamus** and an **elephant** play a game of tug-of-war. As they moved, the field was cleared, ready for planting. Hare's plan worked – all the work had been done and he hadn't moved a muscle!

How the hare got its tail

The animals used to not have tails – just little balls of fluff instead. One day, the lion proposed that they go and get new tails, but Hare was too lazy to go. He asked the animals to **collect a tail** for him, but they refused. The next day, Hare went to collect his tail, but it was too late! Because of his laziness, they had run out. Hare was left with the **fluffy ball** for a tail, forever.

Pool games

There was once a **drought**, so all the animals (except for Hare) tried to get the water back. Eventually, they succeeded and a pool appeared. The animals guarded their pool in case Hare tried to steal their water. Hare tricked some of the animals and took water, but then the tortoise stood guard. He covered his shell with something sticky and hid at the bottom of the pool. With the pool unguarded, Hare jumped in. His **feet stuck** to the tortoise's shell and he was trapped there until the morning.

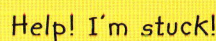

Help! I'm stuck!

Raven

The **Indigenous peoples** of **North America** say Raven has lived on Earth forever — plenty of time to cause mischief!

Confident creator

No bigger than an ordinary raven, this trickster is clever and confident. In folklore, Raven was important in the creation of the world. It is said that he made the **first piece of land** emerge from the oceans.

Raven's actions were sometimes SELFISH but the Indigenous peoples APPRECIATED all he did.

Switched on

When Raven grew tired of darkness, he **stole light** from the heavens and lit up Earth. Although versions of the story vary, Raven found the Sun, the Moon, and all the stars, and gave them pride of place in the sky. Though Raven was still ultimately a thief, everyone loved how light **transformed the world**.

Making mischief

Raven often got up to tricks. He stole food, dirtied water, and pulled out people's hair for his nest. This made Raven unpopular with the Indigenous peoples. His enemy was fellow trickster **Coyote** and they endlessly **pranked each other** to see who was the best.

Prankster's punishment

One day, Raven went too far when he **bit the cheek** of a baby. The other creatures decided to take away his beak. Raven was devastated. When he finally got his beak back, he put it on wrong and it stayed in a **crooked position** forever.

Tengu

These demons come from **Japanese stories**. They are powerful **monster-spirits** that can fly and have magic powers and super strength.

Changing bodies

Descriptions of tengu have changed over time. The earliest were dog-like. Later, they became bird-like. Today's tengu are mostly **human-like**, with red faces and big noses, though they still have feathers.

Bad behaviour

Tengu are known for being bad and they enjoy causing trouble. They particularly like playing tricks on **Buddhist priests**, and can make themselves look like priests in order to do so.

Tengu aren't all bad – they do GOOD THINGS for people, too.

Weather control

These spirits have **magical powers**, including the ability to control the weather. They can make rain fall and thunder clouds rumble. To make the wind blow, they use handheld fans.

Fighting fit

Tengu are trained in **martial arts** – they have incredible fighting skills. Because of this, they are often linked with war. They have been known to kidnap people and carry them off into the sky.

Playing with fire

Tengu like to play with fire. This can cause **problems** when nearby objects are accidentally set aflame!

127

Loki

The **Vikings** had many gods. The god who enjoyed causing problems for his fellow gods was Loki, the trickster.

Shape-shifter

Loki was able to **change shape**, becoming an animal or even another person. This allowed him to hide, listen in on conversations, or make a quick escape. Loki's forms include a falcon, a salmon, a fly, and a horse.

Hard to predict

Sometimes Loki was on the side of the gods, and **helped them**. At other times he was mean, told lies, and broke things. When he made trouble, the other gods often found out, and punished him for it.

Odin

Loki's tricks weren't always funny – some were harmful.

Baldur

Family tree

Loki's parents were **giants**, but he was brought up as a foster brother to Odin, the leader of the Viking gods.

The death of Baldur

Baldur was Odin's son. There was a prophecy about Baldur's death, so his mother made everything on Earth promise not to kill him. However, she missed out the **mistletoe plant**. Loki made a spear from mistletoe and tricked another god into killing Baldur with it. This made the gods angry.

The end of days

Ragnarök is the last battle in Viking stories. It has not happened yet, but is predicted to start because of the death of Baldur. The battle will **destroy the world**. Loki will fight alongside his children and the giants, against the other gods.

Jinn

Sometimes known as genies, jinn are very **powerful beings** from Arabic culture, who are sometimes good and sometimes evil. They appear in many forms in various cultures across the world.

Jinn

In Islamic belief, jinn are spirits that are **invisible to humans**, but live on Earth in every non-living thing, such as the ground and the air. Sometimes they take the form of a human or an animal. They can choose whether to use their power to **do good or to cause harm**.

Hinn

There are old Islamic myths that tell of spirits related to jinn, called hinn. There are a few different ideas about hinn. Some say they are created out of **fire**, some say they take the form of **dogs**, and some say that they work with **angels** to battle jinn.

Ghūls

These human-like relatives of jinn are the scariest of all! Ghūls are said to live in **graveyards** or dark places such as **caves**, where they wait for victims to eat. Although they are always changing their appearance, you can spot ghūls by the one thing they can't change – their **donkey hooves**!

Marids

More wicked relatives of the jinn are marids. These **naughty demons** appear in various Arabic stories. Some stories describe marids spying on angels, while others describe them doing the **opposite** to what they are told. However, they are said to be **easily tricked** by clever humans.

Divs

Many myths from Persia, which is now mostly known as Iran, feature monstrous divs. These huge **human-eating beasts** have fur, horns on their heads, and sharp teeth. They **sleep during the day** and **come out at night**. Sometimes, they change into other things, such as dragons or lions.

Huēhuecoyōtl

The **Aztec** god of music, song, and dance loved a party, but whenever he grew restless, he got up to **mischief**...

Party time!

Huēhuecoyōtl was most often seen as a **dancing coyote**. He was the life and soul of the party, and attracted many admirers. Huēhuecoyōtl was usually shown being followed by a **human drummer**.

Skilled shape-shifter

Huēhuecoyōtl belonged to the **Tezcatlipoca** family of Mexica gods who had **shape-shifting** abilities. He could transform into other animals and many tales see him turn into a woman.

Cruel intentions

Although Huēhuecoyōtl was the perfect party host, he could also be cruel. He often **played tricks** on people to keep himself amused and would **lie** to others to get his own way. Unfortunately, Huēhuecoyōtl never considered the consequences of his actions.

Causing conflict

Huēhuecoyōtl was known to start arguments or even **wars** for entertainment. As a result, many **people died**.

Hermes

All work and no play didn't suit **Greek god** Hermes, who started making **mischief** from the day he was born...

Born trickster

Hermes, the **son of Zeus**, was born in a cave. Just hours after his birth, he killed a tortoise and tied seven strings across its shell to make a lyre, a musical instrument. The same day, he **stole 50 cows** and made them walk backwards so their footprints would be traced to the wrong place.

Lyre made from a turtle shell

Music maestro

Hermes arrived home, hid the cows, and pretended nothing had happened. But his mother, Maia, knew the truth and warned him to behave. He was often accused of trickery by other gods, but Hermes **played sweet music** on his lyre to distract them and avoid punishment.

Sleep song

When Zeus asked his son to slay **Argos**, a giant monster with 100 eyes, Hermes played the most captivating music he had ever played. The music calmed Argos down and he fell into a **deep sleep**. Hermes slayed the monster without having to fight.

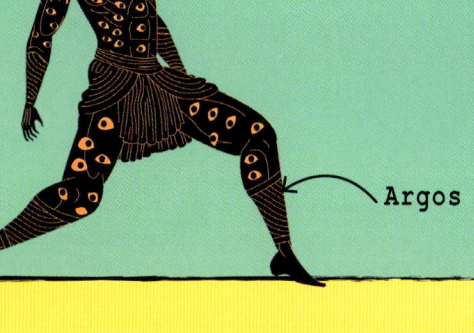

Argos

Winged messenger

As messenger of the gods, Hermes **wore winged sandals** so he could fly. He delivered messages to the living and helped lost travellers find their way. He also carried dead souls to the **underworld**, making Hermes one of only a few gods who could travel between the three realms of the heavens, Earth, and the underworld.

Apollo's golden staff

Winged sandals

Gifts from the gods

Once, Hermes made a reed pipe and played music to Apollo, who liked it so much he asked to keep the pipe. Hermes agreed as long as he could have Apollo's golden staff. This meant Hermes was now **god of shepherds**. His father, Zeus, told him off. Hermes agreed to behave if Zeus made him **messenger of the gods**. Zeus agreed.

Reed pipe

Kitsune

They look a lot like foxes, but kitsune are magical spirits from **Japan**, which can shape-shift. They are known for helping people and teaching lessons to those who have behaved badly.

Shifting shape

Mostly, kitsune appear as foxes. However, they can **change** into human form. Stories describe kitsune becoming old men or young women.

Kitsune are able to control people's minds.

Long life

A kitsune can live for **hundreds of years**. It grows a new tail every 100 years, **up to nine tails**. These change colour as the kitsune ages, starting off red, becoming orange, then changing to gold, before finally becoming white.

Setting the scene

Kitsune can change the **look** of the **place** they are in. That could mean changing a palace into a simple hut, or a dry desert into a lush forest.

Playing tricks

Kitsune often appear in stories as **tricksters**. Their pranks could involve taking human form and marrying a human. A **disguised kitsune** might be spotted if its tail peeks out from under its clothes.

Kitsune disguised as a human

Magic gem

Each kitsune has a hoshi no tama – **a magical gemstone**. This is the source of the kitsune's magic powers. The kitsune keeps hold of the gemstone, as if it **loses the stone**, it loses its magic and dies.

I'm 900 years old!

Some kitsune can FLY and even breathe FIRE!

Sun Wukong

At the heart of **Chinese** mythology is a **warrior monkey** who goes on epic adventures and causes havoc in heaven!

Monkey business

Sun Wukong was a **trickster god** and the leader of other monkeys. He had magical powers and super strength, but this monkey was also quick-tempered, easily distracted, and ready for mischief!

Sun Wukong is also known as the MONKEY KING.

Rocky start

Legend goes that Sun Wukong was born from a **sacred**, **magical rock** when a strong breeze blew. As he was created by the **elements**, he could control wind, fire, earth, and water.

Heavens above

When Sun Wukong tricked the Kings of Hell, he caught the attention of the **Jade Emperor**, who ruled heaven. He invited Sun Wukong to live in his Jade Palace with him.

Prison punishment

But Sun Wukong wasn't happy in heaven, so he started causing trouble. The Jade Emperor sent his soldiers to arrest the monkey, but Sun Wukong defeated them. Buddha imprisoned Sun Wukong beneath a mountain for **500 years**.

Time for change

A passing Buddhist monk offered to free the monkey if he became the monk's bodyguard on a **pilgrimage** to India. Sun Wukong agreed and fought off the monsters they encountered. He changed his ways but remained a great warrior.

Witches

Today, witches are often depicted as cackling characters wearing pointy hats, riding broomsticks, and casting spells over cauldrons. However, there are many **different kinds of witches** from all over the world.

House with chicken legs

Pestle

Mortar

Baba Yaga
Slavic witch Baba Yaga flies around on a **mortar and pestle** usually used to grind up cooking ingredients. She lives with her sisters in a mysterious forest hut that **spins endlessly** on **chicken feet**. Wherever she goes, storms start and **trouble brews**. Her huge appetite is only satisfied by kidnapping, cooking, and eating unfortunate victims she comes across.

Not all witches are bad. In   British myths,

Mother Ludlam

Mother Ludlam was a white witch living in a cave. People would visit her to ask for **any object** they wanted and when they got home, it would be there. Once one man borrowed her cauldron but he never returned it. She was angry, so he hid from her in a church, where the cauldron is said to be today.

Louhi

Finnish queen of witches Louhi controls the Sun and Moon, the weather, and creates new monsters. She waged war for the highly prized **Sampo**, a magical mill that grinds corn, salt, and money. When a rival tried to seize the Sampo, Louhi swooped down to grab it. In the chaos, the Sampo fell to the ocean floor and ground out salt forever more.

Medea

When ancient Greek hero Jason **left Medea** for another woman, she took fatal action. She used her helpful knowledge of potions to coat Jason's new bride's crown and wedding dress in a **killer poison**. The bride died. Delighted with her dark deed, Medea made a quick getaway on a chariot pulled by dragons.

Benevento

This so-called **city of witches** in Italy has been linked to magic since the 13th century. European witches would meet at a great **walnut tree** to cast magic. Whenever they came to Benevento, the branches of the tree filled with **snakes**. A local bishop ordered the walnut tree be chopped down, but it **regrew** every time the witches came back.

Forms and faces

This famous **trickster** can take any form, from a giant to a cheeky little boy or a wise old man. He is always larking about and looking for ways to **stir up trouble**. Despite this, Eshu is mostly good and encourages peace after his mischief-making!

I love to play pranks!

Little boy

Old man

Giant

Eshu

This **playful** god of the Yoruba people in **West Africa** is the master of disguise. He is always causing trouble and mischief!

Causing confusion

Once, Eshu persuaded the Sun and the Moon to **switch places**, leaving the universe in total chaos. He plays tricks on his friends too.

Eshu sometimes has TWO FACES to symbolize

From mayhem to messenger

One day, Eshu took his pranks too far. He stole yams from the **High God's garden** while wearing the High God's slippers. Eshu then blamed the High God for stealing his own yams because his footprints were left behind! The High God punished Eshu by insisting he **visit Earth every day** and report back to him on what had happened there.

Eshu knows all the languages spoken on Earth.

Messenger of the gods

The High God made Eshu the messenger of the gods. Despite his cheekiness, Eshu proved to be an **excellent messenger**. His quick-thinking and protective nature help him deliver messages, prayers, and sacrifices between the gods and the people on Earth.

his love of both chaos and harmony.

Heroes and battles

At the heart of so many myths and legends are brave heroes who strive to **save the day**. Whether they are facing fearsome beasts or fighting enemies on the battlefield, these inspiring heroes are full of **courage**, **strength**, and **determination**.

Trojan War

Among the most famous of all of the **ancient Greek** myths is the enduring story of the ten-year Trojan War.

Love and war

Helen, the Queen of Sparta, was considered the most **beautiful** woman in the world. When she ran away with Prince Paris of Troy, her husband became angry.

Give Helen back!

Never!

Reaping revenge

In revenge, her husband, the King of Sparta, ordered an army of Greek soldiers to attack the **city of Troy**, in what is now Turkey. War raged for a decade and came to an end in the most unexpected way…

Dark horse

The Greek army took Troy by pretending to give up, leaving behind a **large wooden horse** as an offering to the gods. However, soldiers were secretly **hiding** inside the horse. Once the horse was within the city walls, the army jumped out, seized Troy, and took Helen home.

The Trojan Horse was described as being 7 m (23 ft) TALL and 3 m (10 ft) WIDE!

Greek poet Homer

Epic poems

The events of the Trojan War were described by Greek poet Homer in his famous poems **The Iliad** and **The Odyssey**. His accounts were so convincing that many people believed the war was a true story or at least partly based on a historic event.

Fact or fiction

In reality, there are no convincing historical accounts of the Trojan War. Most people recognize it as a classic work of fiction from Greek mythology. But still, you just never know...

Supreme creator

Mahadevi is worshipped in the Hindu religion as the supreme goddess of **creation**. She had **three forms**, each showing her range of abilities and emotions.

Parvati

In this form, Mahadevi is a kind and gentle goddess, symbolizing love and motherhood. She is married to the supreme god Shiva.

Kali

This version sees Mahadevi become Kali, the destroyer goddess. Despite her bloodstained sword and ferocious nature, she is still considered a universal mother to Hindus.

Durga

Mahadevi also becomes Durga, the warrior goddess. She is determined to end evil and protect the people. Her multiple arms hold lots of weapons.

Mahadevi

In this story, the **Hindu** goddess Mahadevi came up against a demon when in her warrior form, Durga. It was a battle to save the world.

Mahishasura

Demonic dictator

Mahadevi was challenged by **Mahishasura**, a shape-shifting demon who wanted to take over the heavens. He was sure he would win as the god Brahma promised **no man** could defeat him.

The name Mahadevi means **"GREAT GODDESS"** in Sanskrit, the sacred language of Hinduism.

Durga

You won't defeat Mahishasura's army!

Mahishasura

Demon's death

A **bloody battle** ensued. Durga's soldiers defeated Mahishasura's armies, enraging him. The two of them fought to the death, when Durga chopped off Mahishasura's head. She had saved the world!

Female force

But **Durga** was no man – she was a warrior goddess! Mahishasura had never encountered her before. She appeared like a force of nature on the back of her lion, armed with weapons given to her by the gods.

149

Inanna in the underworld

A poem, **The Descent of Inanna**, told of how **Sumerian** goddess Inanna braved a visit to the underworld and came face-to-face with death…

Ancient goddess

In ancient Sumer (which is now south-central Iraq), Inanna was goddess of love, wisdom, and war. Her brother, **Utu**, was god of the Sun and truth, while her sister, **Ereshkigal**, ran the Sumerian underworld, called Kur.

Utu

Inanna

Time for a trip

One day, Inanna decided to **visit Kur**. She dressed in her best clothing, protected herself with seven divine powers, and warned her servant to ask the gods for help if she didn't return within three days.

Ereshkigal

Final destination

When she arrived in Kur, Ereshkigal took her sister's clothing and removed all her powers. Inanna assumed she could return to the land of the living, but Ereshkigal and her seven judges **ordered Inanna to die** — no one ever escaped the underworld.

Back to life

When she didn't come back, Inanna's servant asked the gods for help. One god, **Enki**, made two creatures — Kalaturru and Kurgarru — and sent them to rescue Inanna. They sprinkled the water of life on her body and Inanna was revived! She rushed out of Kur and **never returned**.

Kalaturru

Kurgarru

Odin and the wolf

Norse mythology features various deadly battles, including this one between the one-eyed god Odin and Fenrir the wolf.

Freki (and Geri), Odin's wolves

War god

Odin took charge of war and death. His two ravens, **Hugin** ("Thought") and **Munin** ("Memory"), acted as his lookouts, telling him what was happening around the world.

Warring wolves

In Norse mythology, grey wolves are a **symbol of war**. Odin's enemy was a wolf named Fenrir, son of **Loki**. Fenrir had the power to destroy the gods.

A sighting of a GREY WOLF meant

Mjölnir

Thor, the giant-killing god of thunder

Thor

Odin's son Thor was the **god of thunder**. He travelled on a chariot pulled by goats, and carried his trademark hammer, **Mjölnir**. The hammer protected the gods and when thrown, always hit its target.

I gave up my eye in exchange for the power of knowledge.

Hugin (and Munin)

One hungry wolf

The gods crafted a **magical chain** to keep Fenrir at bay. One day, he broke free and swallowed Odin whole. He then ate the Sun and made the world go dark.

Fenrir's freedom

But Fenrir did not get away with killing Odin. In an act of revenge, **Vidar**, Odin's son, stabbed the wolf though the heart. Norse mythology predicted a **whole new world** would arise from all this death and destruction.

good luck on the battlefield.

Sif

Thor's wife was Sif, the **goddess of fertility**. She had flowing golden hair, and she helped farmers by blessing their land with thriving crops. Together, Thor and Sif had two children, **Módi** and **Thrud**, who became adventurers.

Sif, the goddess of fertility

Beowulf and his battles

This **Old English** tale of a hero's battle against three terrifying monsters has captured the imaginations of many.

First foe

Beowulf's first challenge was an ogre named **Grendel**. Beowulf battled the beast, and snapped off one of its arms in the process.

Ultimate hero

Beowulf is from a poem dating back to the **8th century**. He is a brave hero who fights scary monsters.

Beowulf

Beowulf has been translated into more than 60 languages.

Grendel's arm

Reaping revenge

His next rival was **Grendel's mother**, who wanted revenge for her son. Beowulf chopped off her head.

Slaying the dragon

As an elderly king, Beowulf met his final opponent – a **dragon**. He slayed the beast, but the dragon's poisonous bite also killed Beowulf.

Big loss

Everyone went into mourning for their hero. They had lost the **greatest defender** of their kingdom, but they knew that they could live in peace without fearing evil any more.

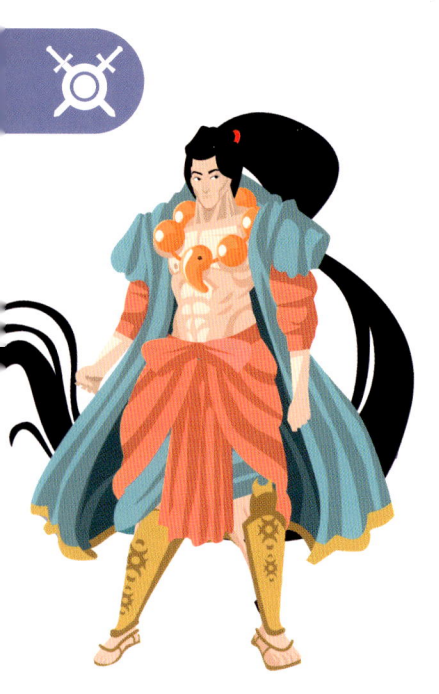

Susanoo and the dragon

This **Japanese** story is about a dragon. Killing the dragon helped the god Susanoo apologize to his sister, the goddess Amaterasu.

Sad news

Susanoo was walking by a river when a **chopstick** floated by. Following where it had come from, he found an **old couple** and their daughter Kushi-nada-hime. They were crying.

Dragon danger

The couple had once had eight daughters, but seven were eaten by the dragon **Yamata-no-Orichi**. The creature had eight heads and eight tails. It was so big that its body crossed eight mountains.

There are SHRINES to Susanoo all over Japan.

Amaterasu

Susanoo was the god of the sea and storms. He argued with his sister, Amaterasu, goddess of the Sun. As a punishment for his bad behaviour, Susanoo was thrown out of heaven and sent to live on Earth.

A clever plan

With the help of the couple, Susanoo **tricked** the dragon into drinking strong alcohol. Yamata-no-Orichi **fell asleep**, and Susanoo quickly sliced it up into little pieces.

Hidden sword

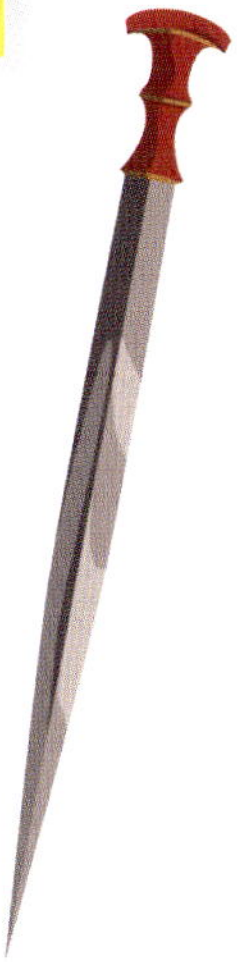

Inside the dragon's body, Susanoo found a **sword**, which he gave to his sister as an **apology**. Susanoo then married and had many children.

As the god of storms, Susanoo controlled winds, thunder, lightning, and the sea.

Fionn MacCumhaill and the Giant's Causeway

The Giant's Causeway is a natural wonder in **Northern Ireland** – and a tale of two warring giants lies behind it…

Fionn MacCumhaill

Giant clash
Legend has it that two giants lived either side of the Irish Sea – **Fionn MacCumhaill** in Ireland and **Benandonner** in Scotland. When Benandonner decided he wanted to take control of Ireland, a battle began!

Bridge to battle
Fionn got angry and **threw rocks** from his coastline into the sea. This created a **path** – the Giant's Causeway – for Fionn to cross the sea and reach Benandonner. But, there was one problem: Benandonner was much bigger than Fionn!

Big baby

Fionn retreated and his clever wife came up with a plan. She **disguised** Fionn as a baby! When Benandonner got to Ireland, he saw the **baby giant**. He realized that if Fionn's baby was this big, then Fionn himself must be huge!

Lucky escape

In a panic, Benandonner quickly ran back to Scotland. On his way home, he **pulled apart pieces** of the path so that it could no longer be used. This resulted in the Giant's Causeway known and loved today.

Benandonner

The Giant's Causeway has been called the EIGHTH WONDER OF THE WORLD.

Giant's Causeway, Northern Ireland

Ancient wonder

Scientists believe that the Giant's Causeway actually formed more than **60 million years ago** when volcanic lava cooled and formed these dramatic pillars. Each column is a hexagonal (six-sided) shape.

Baal's battles

In **Middle Eastern** mythology, Baal waged war with other gods to become the **supreme ruler**.

Storm god

The **ancient Canaanites** of the Middle East worshipped the storm god Baal, who made **thunder** with his mace and **lightning** with his lance. He was responsible for black clouds, torrential rain, and howling winds.

Sea versus storm

When El, King of the Gods, passed on his kingship to the **sea god Yam**, Yam took advantage. He took control of everyone, but Baal challenged him. A mighty battle ensued between the storms and the sea. Armed with magical weapons, Baal killed Yam's sea monsters, and won.

Entering the underworld

As the new ruler, Baal built himself a royal palace on top of Mount Zaphon. However, his peaceful period as King of the gods was short-lived. The **death god Mot** challenged Baal. Mot forced Baal to visit the underworld, and he never returned.

Mot

Back on the throne

After Baal's burial, El **dreamed of Baal** coming back to life. This dream came true as Baal was **suddenly revived**! He rose from the dead, defeated his enemies, and was reinstated as King of the Gods. Even Mot backed down and accepted Baal as leader.

Huitzilopochtli

God of war and Sun, Huitzilopochtli was born for battle. He was the most important god out of more than **200 Aztec gods and goddesses**.

Name game

Huitzilopochtli means "left hummingbird". Legend says the souls of warriors returned as **hummingbirds**. The Aztecs referred to the south, where Huitzilopochtli was from, as the "**left side**" of the world.

Sibling rivalry

Huitzilopochtli is said to have **waged war** from the moment he was born. He was already dressed for battle, armed with a shield of eagle feathers and a snake weapon. He battled his sister, Moon goddess **Coyolxauhqui**, until he cut off her head and threw her down a mountain.

Seeing stars

Before she died, Coyolxauhqui told her **400 brothers** – known as the **Centzon Huitznahua** – to kill their mother. Huitzilopochtli was determined to protect his mother from his brothers. He chased his brothers into the sky where they remained there as the stars of the southern sky. Huitzilopochtli made it his life's work to keep chasing these 400 stars. Aztecs believed this was why the stars moved at night and disappeared as Huitzilopochtli made the Sun rise.

Huitzilopochtli was worshipped at sacred shrines.

All powerful

The Aztecs thought Huitzilopochtli was the most powerful god for many reasons. He represented **the Sun**, which gave light and life. He was the protector of the Aztecs and his courage is said to have helped them to **dominate the battlefield**. He also led them to the special site of **Tenochtitlán**, the Aztec capital city, in 1325 CE. Huitzilopochtli was so important that he was bestowed with gifts, including human sacrifices.

Kintarō

In **Japanese** folklore, Kintarō was a boy whose **limitless strength** and heroic deeds ensured that he is still adored today.

Kintarō means "GOLDEN BOY" in Japanese.

Born winner

Depending on the version told, Kintarō was raised either by his kind mother or a yama-uba ("mountain witch") on **Mount Ashigara**. Even when he was young, Kintarō was strong and courageous. He wrestled bears and pulled trees from the ground with ease.

Wild warrior

Legend goes that Kintarō was descended from a mighty samurai warrior. In many stories he wears bright red and is holding an **axe** in one hand and a **carp** in the other. While living in the mountains, Kintarō befriended a bear, monkey, deer, and hare, and he even learned to talk to these animals!

It's a Japanese tradition to give Kintarō dolls to newborn baby boys.

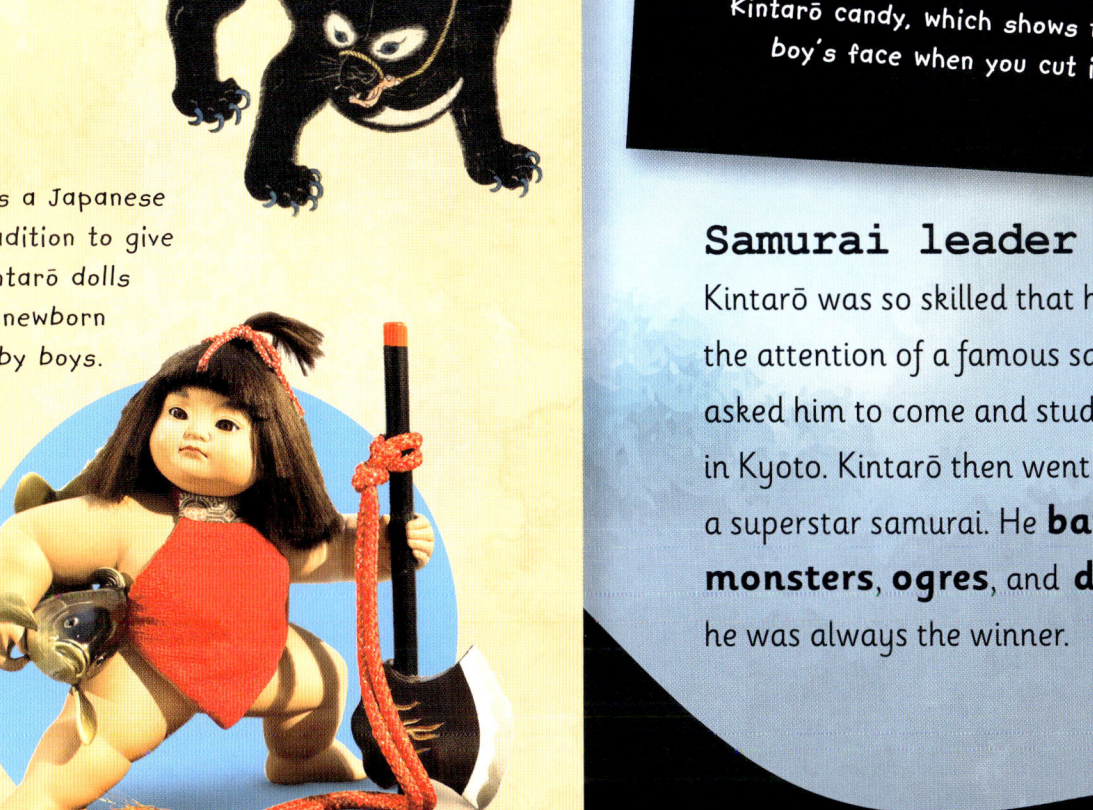

Kintarō is now more popular than ever, and features in modern-day computer games, comics, cartoons, and films. There is even Kintarō candy, which shows the heroic boy's face when you cut into it.

Samurai leader

Kintarō was so skilled that he attracted the attention of a famous samurai who asked him to come and study martial arts in Kyoto. Kintarō then went on to become a superstar samurai. He **battled monsters**, **ogres**, and **demons**, and he was always the winner.

Nüwa saves the world

Nüwa is an **ancient Chinese** creator goddess with the upper body of a human and the lower body of a snake. She brought order to the world after a battle between two gods.

Mother goddess

One ancient Chinese creation myth says that Nüwa created humans out of **clay** and brought them to life because she was lonely. But she realized that people got old and died. She gave humans the ability to have children, so Earth would always have people.

The bottom half of Nüwa's body was that of a slithering snake.

Nüwa and her husband, the god Fuxi, were known as the...

Water against fire

A battle once occurred between water god **Gong Gong** and fire god **Zhu Rong**. Gong Gong was defeated and became angry, hitting his head against one of the pillars that held up the heavens. This tore huge holes in the sky and the world was left overwhelmed by fires and floods.

Mending the heavens

With the world in chaos after Gong Gong and Zhu Rong's great battle, Nüwa stepped in to **save humanity** from destruction.

Holding up the heavens

Nüwa used the legs from a giant tortoise to mend the pillars that held up the heavens.

Nüwa and her husband, Fuxi, had matching snake bodies.

FOUNDERS OF HUMANITY.

Queen Serpot versus Prince Pedikhons

The story of **ancient Egyptian** Queen Serpot and Prince Pedikhons began on the battlefield and proved that love conquers all.

Land of Women

In Egyptian mythology, Queen Serpot reigned over the Land of Women. Here, the women lived together **without men**. They hunted their own food and fought their own wars. This gave them confidence, courage, and independence.

Enemy soldiers

All was peaceful in the Land of Women until one day Queen Serpot **spotted an army** of Egyptian soldiers on the horizon. Leading the way was Prince Pedikhons, who had heard the **legendary stories** of these warrior women and wanted to see them for himself.

This same story was found on an ancient Egyptian PAPYRUS SCROLL told through hieroglyphics.

Battle of the sexes

The two armies went into battle. The Egyptian army fought hard, but the warrior women proved too strong for them. Prince Pedikhons challenged Queen Serpot to a one-on-one duel. She agreed and the two rulers went head to head. As they fought, the prince realized that the queen was **his equal**. The fighting stopped and the two **fell in love**. In the end, love was more powerful than war.

Vaishravana

The king of the north is Vaishravana. He is the **leader** of the Four Heavenly Kings, and **protects Buddhism**. Vaishravana is a skilled warrior, and wears heavy armour. He has power over the **rain**.

Virupaksha

The king of the west is Virupaksha. He is known as the **"one who sees all"**, and is able to look down on Earth, spot those who are not Buddhists, and **help them become Buddhists**.

W

Four Heavenly Kings

Buddhist teachings mention **four gods** who guard the four directions: **north**, **south**, **east**, and **west**. They are known as the Four Heavenly Kings.

Protecting the world

The Four Heavenly Kings have a **very important job**: they **protect the Buddha** and the human world. Each of them protects their own direction, and commands an army of supernatural creatures in the fight against evil.

N

The Four Heavenly Kings are said to live on the lower slopes of Mount Sumeru – a mythical mountain with four sides. It is thought of as the centre of Buddhism.

E

Mount Sumeru

S

Dhritarashtra

In the east is Dhritarashtra. His name means "**upholder of the nation**". Dhritarashtra is a **musician**, and carries a string instrument called a pipa. He uses his beautiful music to encourage people to **become Buddhist**.

Virudhaka

The south's Virudhaka is the **ruler of the wind**. He rides upon a cloud as it floats through the sky above Earth. Virudhaka is a warrior who wears armour and always carries a **weapon**.

Teshub and Illuyanka

This myth is from **Anatolia** in the **Middle East**, an area that is now part of Turkey, but was in the Hittite Empire. It teaches us that everyone needs help sometimes.

An important god

Teshub was the **Hittite** god of weather and storms. Droughts where people did not have enough water to drink were common. So a god who could control the weather and **make it rain** was very important.

Teshub

Illuyanka

A mighty enemy

Teshub was strong and powerful, but he had an **enemy he could not defeat**. This was Illuyanka, a **fire-breathing**, **snake-like dragon**. Being unable to defeat Illuyanka made Teshub very angry. He asked the other gods if they would help him.

The Hittites celebrated Teshub's victory over

Inara and Hupasiya

No god would help Teshub. However, he had a **daughter** named Inara. She was in love with a man called Hupasiya. Together, they came up with a cunning plan to trap Illuyanka. Inara and Hupasiya prepared a great feast, and invited Illuyanka and his family. The dragons ate so much that they **could not fit** through the holes to their underground nests, and drank so much that they **fell asleep**.

Inara and Hupasiya

Inara and Hupasiya served HUGE amounts of food and drink at the feast.

Illuyanka's end

Once Illuyanka was **asleep**, Hupasiya caught him easily. He tied the dragon up so that he was unable to move. Then, finally, **Teshub** was **able to kill** him.

Illuyanka by holding **GREAT FEASTS** every spring.

Mulan

In **ancient China** the story of Mulan is about **bravery on the battlefield**. This inspiring tale is told all across the world.

Venus

The Hua Mulan

Chinese ballad

Many versions of Mulan's story have been told over the years. It all began with a 7th-century poem called the "**Ballad of Mulan**". This ballad was based on a real woman who was extremely brave.

Mulan

I will not let my father fight in the army!

Female fighter

The poem begins with a girl named Hua Mulan. When men were asked to join the army, she decided to take the place of her frail father. She had to pretend to be a man. She wore armour to **disguise her identity** and carried a special sword used by her ancestors.

Secret identity

Mulan became a strong warrior and her real identity went unnoticed. After the war, Mulan was offered an **official role** by the emperor. But she refused, saying she would like to return home to see her family. When she was home, she finally removed her armour, and the other soldiers saw that she was a **woman**.

crater on Venus is named after this CHINESE HEROINE.

At the end

More stories have been written about Mulan, but the ending keeps changing. In one version she fell in love with an officer named **Jin Yong** who knew her true identity. Another tale saw her heading onto the battlefield in women's clothing, revealing her gender to all the other soldiers.

Mulungu

Many African cultures have a **creator god**, and the Bantu peoples know him as Mulungu. He has no clear form and is usually described as being invisible.

Great maker

It is said that Mulungu created the world and keeps watch over it. He is made from all **dead spirits** coming together in one being.

Chameleon

First fire

For a long time, there were no humans on Earth and Mulungu lived **alone**. One day, a chameleon discovered **two humans** caught in a trap and told Mulungu. Mulungu said to wait and see what the people would do before doing anything. One human rubbed sticks together and made a fire, which soon spread. The creatures **took cover** in fear.

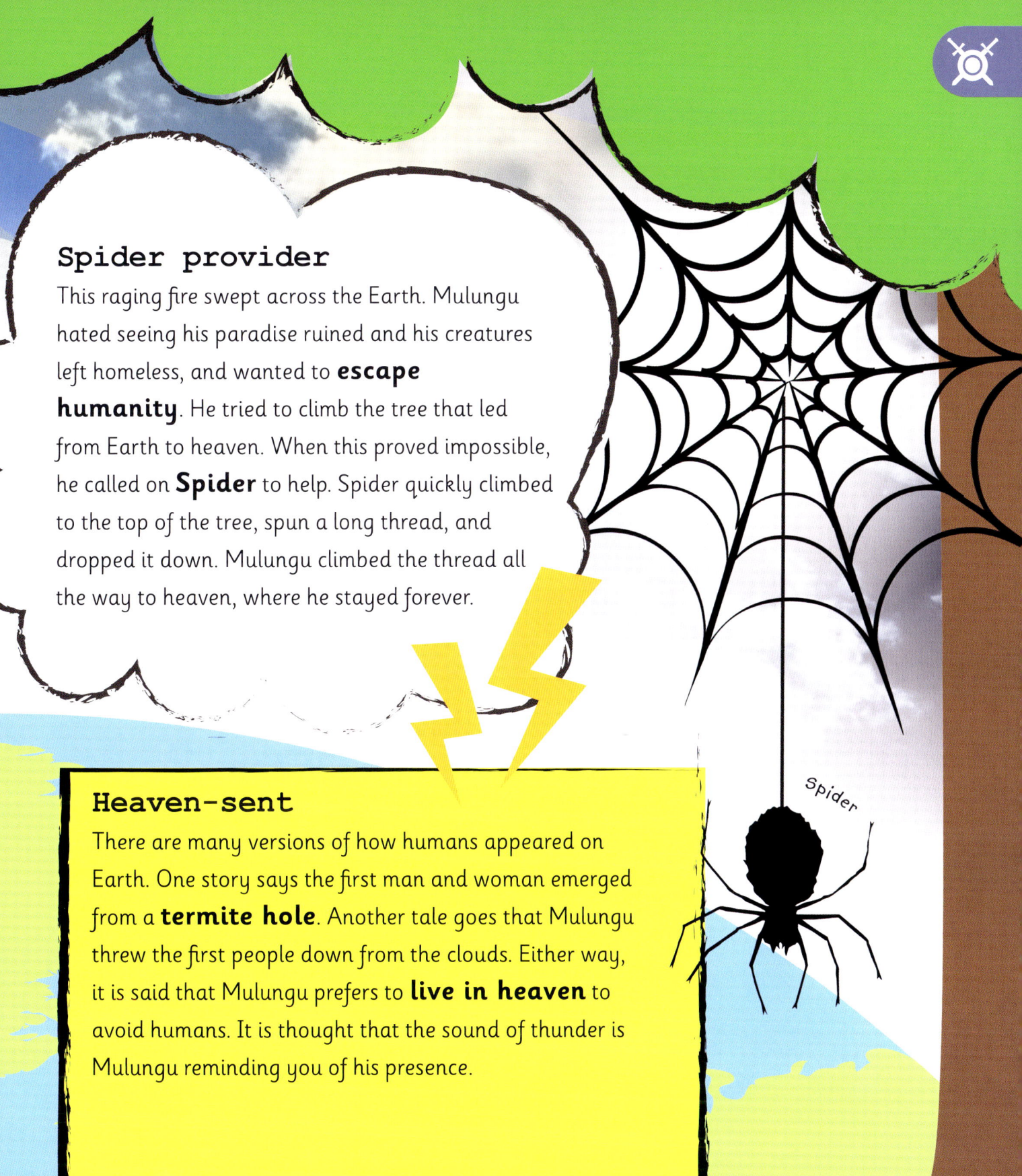

Spider provider

This raging fire swept across the Earth. Mulungu hated seeing his paradise ruined and his creatures left homeless, and wanted to **escape humanity**. He tried to climb the tree that led from Earth to heaven. When this proved impossible, he called on **Spider** to help. Spider quickly climbed to the top of the tree, spun a long thread, and dropped it down. Mulungu climbed the thread all the way to heaven, where he stayed forever.

Spider

Heaven-sent

There are many versions of how humans appeared on Earth. One story says the first man and woman emerged from a **termite hole**. Another tale goes that Mulungu threw the first people down from the clouds. Either way, it is said that Mulungu prefers to **live in heaven** to avoid humans. It is thought that the sound of thunder is Mulungu reminding you of his presence.

Legendary stories

Some stories have really stood the test of time. Their important messages, inspiring characters, and enchanting plots have meant that they have been **shared between communities and cultures** for years. This makes them legendary.

European explorers

In the 16th century, Spanish and Portuguese soldiers known as **conquistadors** were the first Europeans to go to South America. But they murdered many of the people who lived there, took their land, and **stole** their resources such as jewels and gold.

El Dorado

The legend of El Dorado is about a city so rich that it sparkles with gold. This city is said to exist deep in the rainforests of **South America**.

Glittering gold

When the conquistadors heard **stories** about El Dorado, a **city richer** than any other, they wanted to go there. Their plan was to take the precious treasures for themselves...

The city of gold

El Dorado was said to be ruled by a **king** who would cover his whole body in gold dust every morning, then dip into a holy lake to wash it off.

The Amazon rainforest is home to many plants and animals. The people that live there know what is safe and what is not, but the conquistadors had no idea. They ate poisonous plants and were likely attacked by animals such as jaguars and anacondas.

Searching for El Dorado

In **1541**, a group of conquistadors set out on a journey into the **Amazon rainforest.** They hoped to find spices, treasure, and El Dorado. Months later, they returned — they had not found the city, and more than half of them had died on the journey.

Chang'e and the elixir

According to **Chinese legend**, Chang'e stopped a magical potion from falling into the wrong hands…

Sun shooter

There were once ten suns. Their heat was unbearable, so Chang'e's husband, **Hou Yi**, shot down nine of them.

Ten suns

Hou Yi was an expert archer.

Elixir of immortality

Precious gift

With just one sun, the Earth cooled down. Impressed, the goddess **Xiwangmu** gave Hou Yi a potion called the **elixir of immortality**, which would make him live forever. He didn't want to live without his wife, so Hou Yi decided not to drink it, and instead the couple hid it.

Mooncakes

Chang'e

中秋

Self-sacrifice

Hou Yi's evil apprentice **Pángméng** found out that they were hiding the elixir, and ordered Chang'e to hand it over. Not wanting it to get into the wrong hands, Chang'e drank it.

Moonshine

Chang'e was transformed into the **moon goddess**, and floated up into the sky to take her place among the stars. Her husband watched her shining down on Earth until he died.

Chang'e looking down on Hou Yi

Festival favourite

Chang'e is the star of the **Mid-Autumn Festival**, which is celebrated every year in many Asian countries, including China and Vietnam. Family and friends get together to give offerings to Chang'e, including **mooncakes** – pastry cases with a sweet filling.

Fireworks are popular at the Mid-Autumn Festival

Romulus and Remus

The city of Rome, one of the oldest cities in the world, was once at the heart of the ancient **Roman Empire**. Myth says that the city was founded by twin brothers – Romulus and Remus.

Forbidden twins

The twins' mother was human but their father was **Mars**, the god of war. The king ordered a servant to drown them. Instead, the servant put them in a basket on the river, and let them float away.

Mother wolf

Eventually the basket and babies washed up on a river bank. They were found by a **wolf**, who didn't harm them. Instead, she let Romulus and Remus drink milk from her, and cared for the two babies.

Romulus, Remus, and the female wolf

Human parents

After a while, a shepherd and his wife came across the wolf-raised babies. They took the children into their home and **raised them** as their own. The boys grew up and became tall and strong.

Look! Two lovely babies.

Romulus and Remus marched with the heads of the king and his followers on sticks.

Revenge

Once Romulus and Remus became adults, they learnt that the king had tried to kill them when they were babies. They gathered an army and **overthrew** that king.

Rome was eventually built on Palatine Hill, next to the Tiber River.

A new city

Romulus and Remus decided they wanted to found their own city. They argued over where this should be. The arguments became more and more serious, and ended with Romulus **killing his brother**. Romulus then started building Rome.

Romulus

Remus

Romulus was KING of Rome for many years.

Amazon warriors

Legends describe mighty **warrior women** who challenged traditions and fought incredible battles in **Greek** mythology.

The Amazons were great horse riders.

They were skilled archers.

Into battle

In Greek mythology, the Amazons were the **brave daughters** of the war god, **Ares**. These warrior women lived far from any city and were well-trained fighters who wore armour that was stronger than steel.

Fearless fighters

The Amazons are thought to have formed their own nation, **free from men**, so that they could become warriors. They dedicated their lives to fighting and were stronger than most people in Greece. The Amazons stood up to demigods, kings, and nations.

> We don't need men. We can be warriors, too.

Power struggle

The Amazons became famous fighting bloody battles against legendary Greek heroes. Unfortunately, there are very few reports of them ever actually **winning wars against men**. Some say this is because men wrote their stories down and they didn't want to be seen losing to women!

The discovery of hundreds of GRAVES of women warriors suggest there may be some truth to the AMAZON LEGEND.

The Amazon warriors also came up against the Gorgons, a group of women who lived nearby. The Amazons attacked the Gorgons to protect their friends the Atlanteans. The two armies fought for weeks, but eventually the Amazons used their ruthless combat, cunning, and strength to defeat the Gorgons.

Fountain of Youth

Throughout history, explorers have searched for a magical fountain whose waters were said to **restore youth**.

Wonder of water

In many cultures, water is seen as a **healer of sickness** and a symbol of **rebirth**, so lots of people believed in the fountain. Drinking or bathing in its waters was said to make people young again.

> Wow! You look good for 120 years old!

> Yes, isn't it magical? The fountain made me young again!

First fountain

In the 5th century BCE, Greek writer **Herodotus** wrote about people who lived for 120 years! They claimed to bathe in a fountain that made their skin smooth and shiny.

Herodotus

Quest for youth

Alexander the Great looked unsuccessfully for a **magic river** to heal his body as he got older. Spanish explorers were told about a similar river, but they didn't find it either.

Caribbean river

Alexander the Great

Tourist trap

Explorer Juan Ponce de León looked for the Fountain of Youth in the 16th century. He searched **Florida** in the USA and **Bimini** in the Bahamas but never found it.

Fountain of Youth tourist attraction, Florida, USA

Modern cure

The Fountain of Youth was never found, but healing **hot springs** are found around the world, including Japan, Iceland, and Chile.

Macacques enjoy the hot springs in Japan.

189

Knights of the Round Table

For centuries, children have been reading the **British** tales of **King Arthur** and his knights.

Classic story

The stories of *King Arthur and his Knights of the Round Table* feature a powerful king, a huge castle, a mystical magician, and big battles. The characters in the stories are based on real **Medieval knights**.

Brave knights on horseback

The sword was called Excalibur.

Sword in the stone

Legend goes that the magician **Merlin** sank a special sword into a stone and whoever pulled it out would become king. Hundreds tried, but **nobody was strong enough** – until a boy named Arthur removed the sword.

Some historians believe KING ARTHUR was

King's knights

King Arthur lived in a castle called **Camelot**, where he was joined by more than 150 knights. They protected the king and kept the peace. King Arthur married a woman called Guinevere, whose father gave him a **round table** for his knights to sit at.

King Arthur and the Knights of the Round Table

Holy Grail

According to the Christian Bible, the Holy Grail was a **sacred cup** that Jesus Christ drank from. It was said to have magical powers and cure all illnesses. Many of King Arthur's knights tried and failed to find the Holy Grail. **Sir Galahad** was the only one to see it before he ascended to heaven.

Sir Galahad kneeling at the sight of the Holy Grail

Holy Grail

a real warrior from the 6TH CENTURY.

Pandora's jar

In **ancient Greek** mythology, the gods gave Pandora a gift that would cause trouble for humanity.

First woman's gift from the gods

The Greek gods created Pandora, making her the first woman on Earth. Pandora means "**all gifts**", so the gods presented her with gifts. These gifts were stored inside a jar, called "**pithos**" in Greek. Pandora was told that she must never, ever open the jar.

Pandora's jar

What's inside?

Pandora couldn't help being **curious**. She kept looking at the jar and wondering what was inside. One day, curiosity got the better of her, and she decided to **open the jar**.

Evil unleashed

As Pandora opened the lid, a rush of **evil spirits** spilled out into the world. In horror, she tried to shut the lid, but it was too late. Only **hope remained** inside the jar. It turned out that the gods wanted to punish people on Earth to make them listen to the gods.

Hope safely stayed in the jar, which meant

All evil spirits, such as war and flooding, escaped from the jar.

Oh no! I wish I had never opened this jar!

Over time, Pandora's jar has been mistranslated as a box. People now use the phrase "opening Pandora's box" to describe creating many problems from one action.

Life lessons

The tale of Pandora's jar is thought to **teach humans** a few lessons. Pandora was warned not to do something, but she gave in to curiosity and paid the price. This myth shows that humans should respect decisions made by others, and that sometimes being nosy can make things worse. But it also unfairly blames women for bad things that happen in the world.

that humankind would ALWAYS HAVE HOPE.

Ranginui and Papatūānuku

In the **Māori** legends, the love between the Sky Father and the Earth Mother led to the creation of the world.

Earth and sky

The Māori are the indigenous people of New Zealand. Ranginui, the **Sky Father**, was their god of the sky and the heavens. Papatūānuku, the **Earth Mother**, was their goddess of all the land.

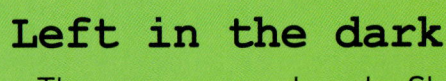

Would it be easier to see if there was light?

Left in the dark

The story starts when the Sky Father and the Earth Mother hugged each other. This blocked the light and the world was then in total darkness, known as **Te Pō**. The couple shared **six sons**, who grew up in the dark. As the sons grew up, they talked about what the light might be like.

Unbreakable bond

The sons tried to separate their parents to let in the light. They tried to push Ranginui into the **sky overhead**, and Papatūānuku to the **ground below**, but it was no good. They couldn't break their parents apart.

Force of nature

Eventually, one of the sons, the forest god **Tāne Mahuta**, forced them apart. Light flooded in. The sons celebrated, but the wind god **Tāwhirimātea**, hated seeing his parents sad. He joined his father in the sky.

Endless love

This love story is still told today, and the Māori believe that we can see the couple's sadness in nature. Rain and morning dew are **Ranguini's tears**, while mist is **Papatūānuku sighing** for her lost love. But their heartbreak meant that everyone else could live in lightness.

Aladdin

The story of Aladdin starts with an ordinary young boy. A wicked magician sent him into a **magical cave** to seek a precious lamp, which changed Aladdin's life forever.

A certain boy

One day, an evil magician learned about a **cave** full of **precious treasures**. However, it could only be opened by one person – Aladdin. The magician searched all over the world to find him.

The treasure cave

Once he found him, the magician persuaded Aladdin to go into the cave to get a **golden lamp**. Aladdin crept through the cave. Eventually, he found the lamp, but he became trapped in the cave.

I am the slave of the lamp! Tell me what you wish for!

A magical lamp

Terrified, Aladdin rubbed the lamp and a **magical genie** suddenly emerged! He granted Aladdin's wishes, sending him home and making him very rich.

Princess Badr al-Badur

One day, Aladdin spotted the emperor's daughter, **Princess Badr al-Badur**. He went to meet the emperor and begged to **marry** her. Aladdin was so rich that the emperor agreed. From afar, the evil magician saw Aladdin and the princess, and became very jealous.

A happy ending

The magician ordered his magical slave to take **Aladdin's palace** and hide it. However, Aladdin tracked down the palace and, with his wife's help, he outwitted the magician.

Aladdin and the princess lived happily after, and he eventually became EMPEROR.

The Arabian nights

Aladdin is one story from a collection known as the *Arabian Nights*, or the *One Thousand and One Nights*. These stories are from the **Middle East**, and were told for many years before they were ever written down.

Obatala and the creation of Ife

In the **Yoruba** beliefs of **West Africa**, Obatala created humankind, but it didn't quite go according to plan!

Lay of the land

The Yoruba people believe that Olódùmarè is the **supreme god** in charge of the entire universe. Olódùmarè chose fellow god Obatala to make Earth.

Stories say that the ancient city of Ife in modern-day Nigeria was created by Obatala.

ZzZzzz

Zzz

Clay humans

Next, Obatala was asked to create humanity from clay. But he got **sleepy** and began drinking palm wine instead.

Protector of people

Olódùmarè was disappointed with Obatala's efforts and sent down another god, **Oduduwa**, to help. Obatala awoke to find Oduduwa had taken charge of humanity. But Obatala didn't give up. He strived to protect and help those **weakest** and **most vulnerable** in society to make up for his own carelessness.

For a while, Obatala ruled Ife, bringing CALM and ORDER to the land he created.

I did not steal that horse!

False accusation

At one point, Obatala was **wrongly accused** of stealing a horse and was sent to prison for seven years. Without his leadership, Ife went through years of conflict, famine, and disease. When Obatala was released from prison, peace was restored. To this day, the Yoruba people worship him because he represents **care and compassion**.

The Trimurti

At the heart of the **Hindu** religion is the Trimurti, **three forms of god** worshipped by followers of this faith.

Hindu trinity

Hindus have a single, supreme god who has three forms or faces: **Brahma** the creator, **Vishnu** the preserver, and **Shiva** the destroyer.

A picture of the Trimurti at Jagannath Temple, Odisha, India

There are about 1.2 BILLION Hindus worldwide.

Brahma
The Hindu **creator of the universe** is Brahma. His four heads can see in every direction. Some stories say he was born from a golden egg, while others say he came from a **lotus flower** that bloomed from Vishnu's belly button. Brahma went on to make the universe and everything in it.

Vishnu

The **preserver of the universe** is Vishnu, who represents **power** and **enlightenment**. He keeps order and maintains the balance between good and bad. Two of his four arms are at the front, in the human world, and the two at the back are in the spiritual world. His arms carry symbolic objects – a **conch shell**, a **chakra (wheel)**, a **club**, and a **lotus flower**.

The name Trimurti is Sanskrit for "three forms".

Shiva

The **destroyer of the universe** is Shiva. His four arms hold a **drum**, a **trident (spear)**, a **flame**, and a **pen**. Although he is an angry god whose role of destroyer sounds terrifying, Hindus believe destruction is followed by new things being created. This means that each time Shiva destroys the universe, it is reborn.

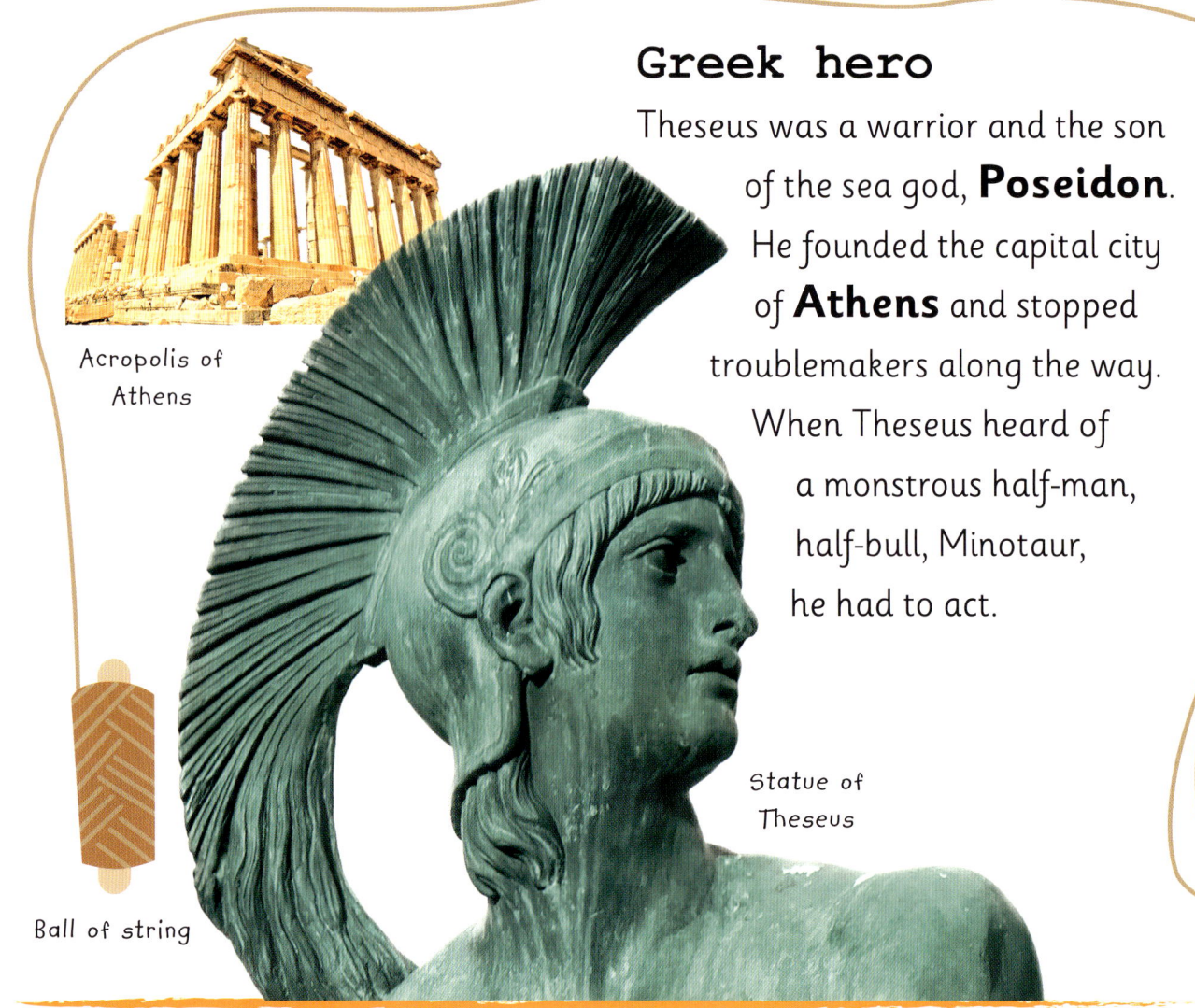

Greek hero

Theseus was a warrior and the son of the sea god, **Poseidon**. He founded the capital city of **Athens** and stopped troublemakers along the way. When Theseus heard of a monstrous half-man, half-bull, Minotaur, he had to act.

Acropolis of Athens

Statue of Theseus

Ball of string

Theseus and the Minotaur

Ancient Greece was the scene for this ultimate showdown. In this tale, a **legendary hero** saved the island of Crete from a terrifying creature.

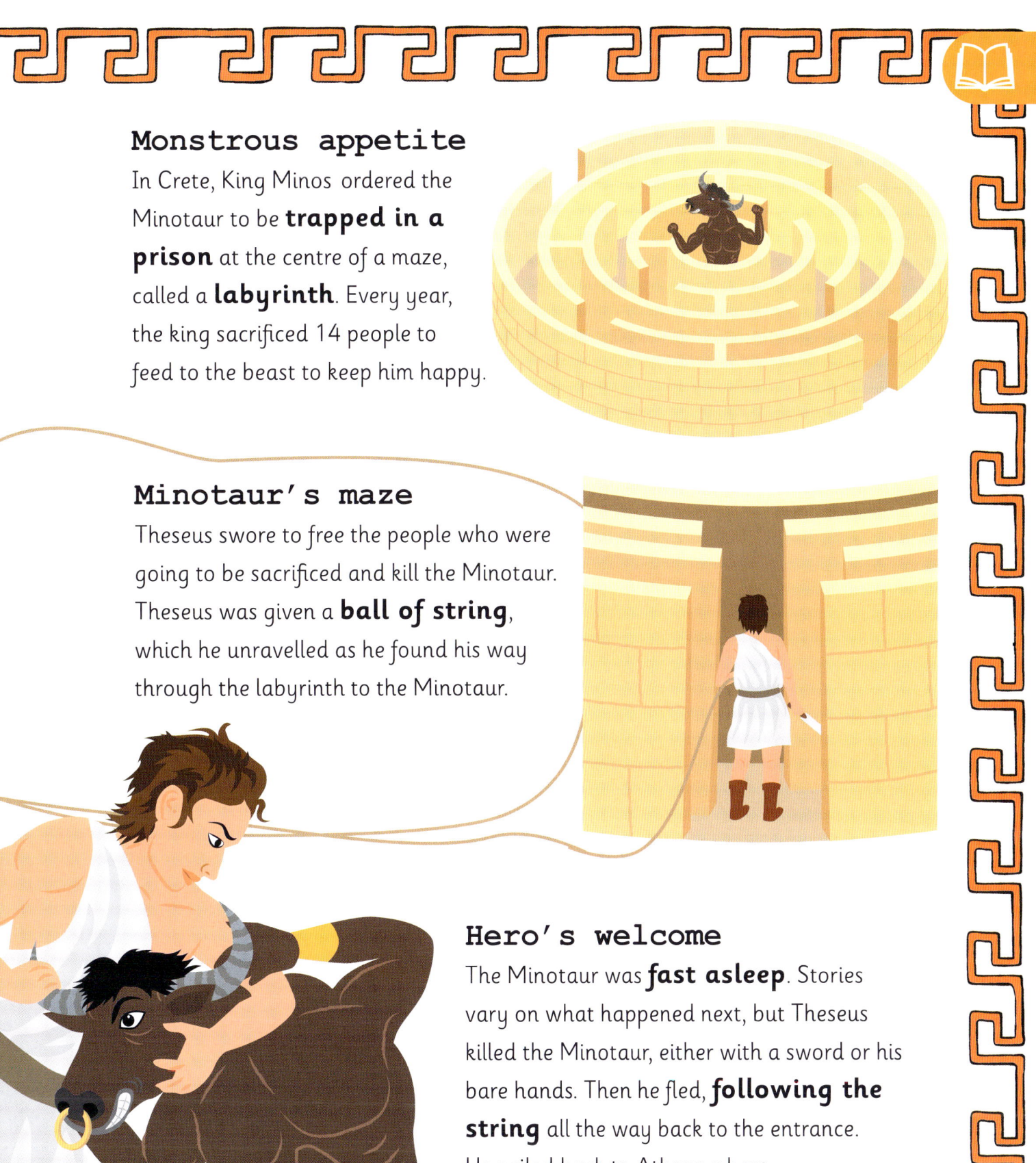

Monstrous appetite

In Crete, King Minos ordered the Minotaur to be **trapped in a prison** at the centre of a maze, called a **labyrinth**. Every year, the king sacrificed 14 people to feed to the beast to keep him happy.

Minotaur's maze

Theseus swore to free the people who were going to be sacrificed and kill the Minotaur. Theseus was given a **ball of string**, which he unravelled as he found his way through the labyrinth to the Minotaur.

Hero's welcome

The Minotaur was **fast asleep**. Stories vary on what happened next, but Theseus killed the Minotaur, either with a sword or his bare hands. Then he fled, **following the string** all the way back to the entrance. He sailed back to Athens a hero.

Hlakanyana

Among many African trickster tales are the **Bantu** peoples' tales of Hlakanyana. This **shape-shifting** child uses cleverness and cunning to cause mischief in the community.

Total trickster

Hlakanyana loves to play tricks and often escapes capture by taking **different forms** – whether that be a boy or girl, or even an animal.

All in a stew

In one story, Hlakanyana appears as a girl who plays a game with an old lady – and the lady ends up in a **pot of stew**! Then Hlakanyana serves the stew to the villagers. They are **horrified** when they find out the lady was in the stew, and search for Hlakanyana. But Hlakanyana has transformed into a rock so they escape punishment.

Bread thief

In another tale, Hlakanyana comes across a monster eating a **loaf of bread**. Hlakanyana steals the bread and the monster grabs their leg. But the monster is tricked into thinking the leg is a **tree root** and lets go. Once again, Hlakanyana goes free and gets away with their crime.

Payback time

Another time, Hlakanyana makes a **whistle** to play music. An iguana hears the melody and asks to borrow the whistle. Hlakanyana agrees, but the iguana **steals it**. Hlakanyana never forgets this and later returns to kill the iguana and take back the whistle.

Burned out

In a tragic story, Hlakanyana comes home carrying a **tortoise** on their back. The tortoise won't let go, so Hlakanyana's mother has to pour **boiling fat** over the tortoise to get it off. But some of the fat lands on Hlakanyana and burns them.

Shipwrecked sailor

This **ancient Egyptian** story is about a sailor who gets stuck on a desert island and is looked after by a huge golden snake. The story has a hidden meaning: that happiness can be found at home with your family.

A young sailor went to sea on a ship with a crew of 120 people. One day, a terrible storm hit the ship. Waves crashed across the deck, and the sailor was washed overboard and into the ocean.

When the sailor woke up, he was completely alone on the sandy shores of a desert island. Scared, he took shelter under a tree, and made a fire to keep himself warm.

Evidence suggests that this STORY dates back to 2000-1900 BCE.

3

Suddenly, a gigantic golden snake appeared from a nearby forest. Its scales sparkled and its eyebrows were made of precious stone. The snake picked the sailor up and carried him away.

4

The snake didn't harm him. Instead, it asked him why he had travelled to the island. The sailor said he had never meant to visit the island and had been stranded there by a storm.

5

The snake told the sailor that it had lost its own family when a star fell from the sky and burned them up. It promised that the sailor would see his family again. In the meantime, it would make sure that he was looked after.

6

Several months later, a boat arrived. The sailor asked the snake, "How can I thank you?". The snake replied, "Enjoy your family for me once you get back to them. Hug them, and tell them how much you love them."

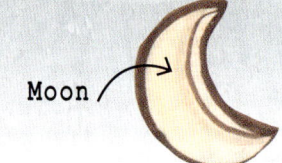

Moon

The churning of the ocean

In this **Hindu creation myth**, a number of important treasures are found, including the Sun and the Moon. It is one of many stories about the struggle between the gods and the demons.

Vishnu

Endless life

One day, the gods and demons gathered. They wanted to find the **elixir of immortality**. The problem was, the elixir was hidden somewhere on the ocean floor.

Mount Mandara

The gods (or Devas) trying to churn the ocean.

208

Mixing it up

The god **Vishnu** suggested that they should try to churn the ocean – mixing it up until the elixir was forced out. They used **Vasuki** the snake as a rope and **Mount Mandara** as a massive paddle. Working together, the gods and demons wrapped Vasuki around the paddle. They then pulled him back and forth to make the paddle turn. Soon the water became milky and then turned to butter.

Sun

Vasuki

Precious objects

As the gods churned, **14 precious things** appeared. They included the **Sun**, the **Moon**, and goddess **Lakshmi**. Last to appear was the elixir of immortality.

Vishnu and Lakshmi got married.

Drinking the elixir

Vishnu distracted the demons so that the gods could drink the elixir and become immortal. Only one of the demons got to take a sip. Vishnu quickly **cut off its head**, but it didn't die and declared war.

The demons (or Asuras) working with the gods.

Demon's immmortal head

Pan Gu

Have you heard the story about a mysterious man who hatched from an egg before time began? In **ancient China**, Pan Gu was the first being in the universe and the creator of all the world.

Cosmic egg

Pan Gu was the very **first being**. He was created inside a giant egg, where he slept for 18,000 years. Around him, the forces of Yin and Yang fought against each other, causing chaos and conflict.

Pan Gu is sometimes shown holding a hammer to break the egg.

Cracked open

Eventually, the egg cracked and Pan Gu pushed the shell apart. **Yin and Yang** were separated, finally finding a balance with each other. Pan Gu stood there with two horns and a body covered in hair. The top of the shell became the **sky** and the bottom part made **Earth**.

Taking shape

Some legends say Pan Gu started hammering and chiselling to **create the universe**. He shaped the Sun, Moon, stars, and planets, ordered the seas, and dug out valleys. Others say he was helped by an **army of creatures**, including a dragon, a phoenix, a qilin, and a tortoise.

The Zhuang people of China still sing a song about Pan Gu creating HEAVEN and EARTH.

Yin and Yang

In Chinese philosophy, Yin symbolizes the feminine, dark, and negative, and Yang the masculine, light, and positive. These two forces cause **conflict** if they collide, but if they stay apart, they create **harmony**.

The Sun's daughter

This legend, from the **Cherokee** people of **North America**, tells us of what happened when the Sun shone too bright.

Burning Sun

The Sun was **jealous** of the Moon so she began to burn brighter. The world became so hot that people started to **die**. Desperate, the people decided to kill the Sun.

Beloved daughter

The Sun had a daughter, whom she loved very much. Every day the Sun would journey across the sky, stopping at her **daughter's house** for lunch. The people knew this, and used it in their plan.

The wait begins

The people turned two men into **poisonous snakes** – a Spreading Adder and a Copperhead. They then waited for the Sun to arrive at her daughter's house. But, the Sun's brightness blinded them and they couldn't get near her.

Copperhead

An accidental death

So, the people **tried again**. This time one man became a **Rattlesnake**, and another a **Uktena** snake. As the door to the house opened, the Rattlesnake rushed inside and bit and killed the first person he saw – the Sun's daughter.

Uktena

Rattlesnake

Spreading Adder

A dark world

The Sun was so sad that she shut herself away from the world, and it became **cold and dark**. The people worried that without the Sun's light, Earth would die. So, they tried to bring her daughter back from the dead.

In the box

The people visited the land of the dead, called the **Darkening Land**. They found the Sun's daughter there, and put her in a box. Eventually, she tricked them into opening the box, turned into a **redbird**, and flew away.

Happy drums

The Sun was **so sad** that she cried floods. The people tried to make her happy. One day a drummer began playing a funny beat, and the Sun finally **started to smile again**. Her light has been burning ever since.

The death of Osiris

This **ancient Egyptian** story tells of how the god-king Osiris went from being king of the living to king of the dead. His wife, **Isis**, also made him into the first ever mummy.

Isis

Osiris

Ancient Egyptians believed the

Rulers of Egypt

King Osiris and his wife, Isis, ruled over the people of Egypt. They were **wise** and **fair** rulers. They also taught their people how to farm wheat and barley.

A jealous brother

Osiris's brother **Set** was jealous of Osiris and wanted to be king himself. He tricked Osiris into climbing inside a beautiful chest. Then he had the chest thrown into the **Nile River**, with Osiris's body still inside.

Set

Isis to the rescue

Heartbroken, Isis searched the Nile for the chest, before finding it trapped in the **roots of a tree**. She took it home and hid it in the **sand dunes**. She decided to keep it safe until she could find a magical way to bring Osiris back to life.

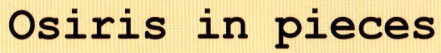

Osiris in pieces

The next day, Set discovered the chest. He smashed it open, and ripped Osiris' body into tiny pieces. Set then travelled all over Egypt, **scattering pieces** of the body as he went.

yearly NILE FLOODS were caused by Isis crying for her husband.

Isis's search

Isis searched for the pieces, with the help of Set's wife, **Nephthys**. They found most of the pieces, then used magic and bandages to put the body back together and bring Osiris **back to life**.

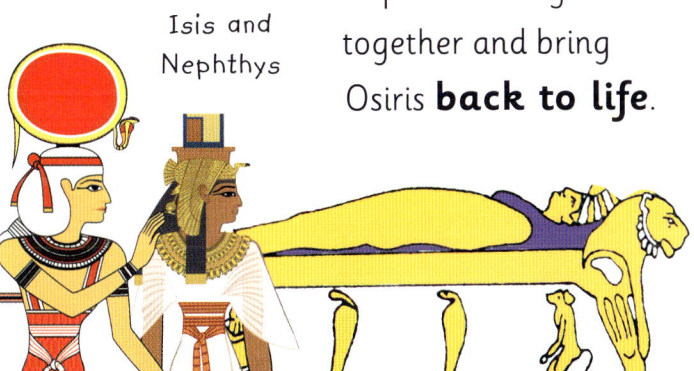

Isis and Nephthys

King of the dead

Osiris and Isis had a son together – **Horus**. Osiris then moved to the **land of the dead**, where he became king. Horus grew up protected by his mother. As an adult, he defeated his uncle Set, becoming the King of Egypt.

Horus

Pronunciation guide

Use this handy list to find out **how to say** the names of the mythical creatures and legends in this book.

Aladdin
a-LAD-in

Amaterasu
a-ma-teh-RA-soo

Ammit
AH-mit

Anansi
an-AN-see

Baal
BAYL

Baba Yaga
BA-ba YA-ga

Banshees
BAN-shees

Basilisks
BA-suh-lisks

Benevento
beh-nuh-VEN-tow

Beowulf
BAY-oh-wulf

Brahma
BRAA-mah

Brownies
BROW-nees

Bunyip
BUN-yip

Butzemanns
but-ZEH-mans

Chalchiuhtlicue
chal-CHEE-weet-lee-kway

Chang'e
CHAHNG-uh

Charybdis
ka-RIB-dis

Chimera
kai-MEER-a

Coyote
kai-YOH-tee

Cuca
KOO-kah

Dakuwaqa
DAH-coo-wah-kah

Dhritarashtra
dri-tah-RASH-tra

Divs
DIVS

Dokkaebi
DOH-keh-bih

El Hombre Del Saco
el OM-bray del SA-ko

El Dorado
el duh-RAH-doh

Elves
ELVZ

Encantados
in-kan-TAH-dohs

Eshu
EH-shoo

Fáfnir
FAF-ner

Fionn MacCumhaill
FIN ma-KOOL

Ganga
GAN-gah

Gargouille
gar-GOIL

Garuda
ga-ROO-dah

Ghūls
GU-ls

Griffins
GRIF-ins

Hare
HAIR

Harpies
HAR-pees

Hermes
HER-meez

Hinn
HIN

Hlakanyana
hey-lah-KAN-yan-nah

Huēhuecoyōtl
way-way-COH-yoh-tl

Huitzilopochtli
HWIT-zil-uh-pohch-lee

Hydra
HAI-dra

Illuyanka
il-loo-YAN-kah

Imps
IMPS

Inanna
ih-NAH-na

Jinn
JIN

Kāmohoali'i
ka-MO-ho-ah-lee-ee

Kappas
KAP-pahs

King Arthur
King AR-thur

Kintarō
kin-TAH-roh

Kitsune
KIT-soo-nay

Kraken
KRAK-en

Kuzuryū
KU-zur-ee

Leprechauns
leh-PRUR-kawns

Leviathan
leh-VAI-ah-than

Loch Ness monster
LOCH ness MON-stuhr

Loki
LOW-kee

Louhi
LOH-ee

Lumaluma
LOO-mah-loo-mah

Mahadevi
MA-ha-deh-vi

Maman Dlo
MA-mon DLOH

Mami Wata
MA-mee WHA-tah

Marids
MAH-rids

Maui
MOW-ee

Medea
meh-DEE-a

Medusa
meh-DOO-sah

Mermaids
meh-MAYDZ

Mother Ludlam
MUH-ther LUD-lam

Mulan
MOO-lan

Mulungu
mu-LUN-goo

Namahage
na-ma-HA-gay

Nian
NEE-yan

Ninki Nanka
NIN-kih NAN-ka

Nüwa
NYOO-wa

Obatala
oh-BA-ta-la

Odin
OH-din

Osiris
Oh-SAI-ris

Pan Gu
pahn-GOO

Pandora
pan-DOR-ah

Papatūānuku
pa-pa-too-a-NOO-koo

Pedikhons
PED-ee-kons

Pegasus
PEG-a-suss

Phoenixes
FEE-nixes

Pixies
PIK-sees

Qallupilluit
kah-loo-PIL-lu-it

Qilins
CHEE-linns

Ra
RAR

Rainbow Snake
RAYN-boh sneyk

Rán
RAN

Ranginui
RANG-ih-noo-ee

Raven
RAY-vuhn

Remus
REE-muhs

Rocs
ROKS

Romulus
ROM-ye-luss

Ryūjin
RYOO-jin

Saci-pererê
SA-si-peh-reh-ray

Scylla
SILL-ah

Serpot
SER-pot

Shiva
SHEE-vah

Sirens
SAI-rens

Sprites
s-PRITE-s

Sun Wukong
SON wuh-KONG

Susanoo
soo-sa-NO

Taniwha
tan-ee-WAH

Tengu
TEN-goo

Teshub
TEH-shub

Theseus
THEE-see-us

Thunderbird
THUN-dur-burd

Tiamat
TEE-uh-mat

Tokoloshes
tohk-oh-LOHSH-s

Trimurti
TRAI-mur-tee

Ukko
UK-oh

Unicorns
YOO-nih-korns

Vaishravana
VAI-shra-vah-nah

Vampires
VAM-pai-ers

Virudhaka
vir-oo-DAH-kah

Virupaksha
vir-oo-PAHK-sha

Vishnu
VISH-noo

Werewolves
WAIR-wolvz

Wewe Gombel
WAY-way GOM-bel

Yacumama
YA-koo-mah-mah

Yara-ma-yha-whos
yara-meh-AH-whos

Yetis
YEH-tees

Myths **words**

This book is filled with words relating to myths. Some can be a bit tricky, so if you ever get stuck, look here.

Ancestor A person from whom someone is descended, such as a great-grandmother.

Constellation A group of stars in the sky that follow a pattern and are named after an animal or mythical person.

Creation The way the Universe was created.

Demigod Someone who is part god and part human.

Demon A creature or spirit that does evil.

Dreamtime A period of time in the First Nations religion, when powerful spirits created life and shaped the land into the form seen today.

Elixir of immortality A potion believed to be able to extend a person's life forever, making them immortal.

Epic Long and difficult.

Eternity Forever.

Fertility Ability to create life, from fertile land for crops to fertile animals.

Folklore/folk tales Traditional beliefs and stories that have been passed on for many years, by word of mouth.

God Male supernatural being, worshipped due to their great powers.

Goddess Female supernatural being, worshipped due to their great powers.

Havoc Destruction.

Heaven A place above the sky that is believed to be the home of the gods, or a place where the spirits of good people go after death.

Hurricane A violent storm.

Immortal Unable to die.

Indigenous Referring to peoples who lived in an area before any settlers arrived.

Legend A mythical story from the past, telling of a famous deed or action.

Mischief Trouble that is not meant to cause serious harm.

Myths Ancient stories that explain history. They are often about the nature of the world, and often contain supernatural characters.

Narratives Stories

Omen An event that is seen as a sign of good or evil.

Prophecy A prediction of what could happen in the future.

Prosperity Wealth.

Sacrifices The killing of people or animals, as part of a religious ceremony.

Samurai A Japanese warrior.

Serenity Peace.

Serpent A large snake.

Shape-shift The ability to look like other creatures or objects.

Shrines Places where people worship a god, holy person, or event.

Spirits Magical beings without physical form, or the souls of people.

Supernatural Actions or forces that are beyond the laws of nature.

Supreme The greatest.

Symbol Something that stands for something else.

Toxic Poisonous.

Transform Change.

Trickster Someone who likes to play jokes on others, or cheat them out of things.

Underworld Mythical land of the dead, imagined to be under the ground.

Vengeance Revenge.

Witch A woman with magical powers.

Worship Showing love and respect for a god.

Index

Acknowledgements

DK would like to thank: Laura Gilbert for proofreading, and Vanessa Bird for compiling the index.

The publisher would like to thank the following for their kind permission to reproduce their photographs:

(Key: a-above; b-below/bottom; c-centre; f-far; l-left; r-right; t-top)

1 Dorling Kindersley: NASA (tl). Dreamstime.com: Pavel Naumov (cl/Tornado); Ihor Svetiukha (cla); Alina Pavlovska (tc). Getty Images / iStock: drmakkoy (c); Luiz Felipe Goncalves (cl); ain_mikail (cr). 2 Shutterstock.com: Antracit (cra). 3 Alamy Stock Photo: Oleg Zhukov / YAY Media AS (ftl). Dorling Kindersley: NASA (crb). Dreamstime.com: Surabhi25 (tr). Getty Images / iStock: Elena Belous (cla); VectorUp (tl); ain_mikail (cl); VasjaKoman (clb); SpicyTruffel (br). 4 123RF.com: Svetlana Yefimkina (t). Dreamstime.com: Makhnach (tl). Getty Images / iStock: eurobanks (bl, br); HeyHeyDesigns (t/Fairies); JDawnInk (br/Fish). 4-5 Dreamstime.com: Benchart (bc). Getty Images / iStock: Roman Kulinskiy (t). 5 123RF.com: ramiraise (bl/book). Dreamstime.com: Olga Ermolaeva (bl/Gold eggs); Boris Zerwann (bl); Jan Martin Will (crb); Ominaesi (cra). Getty Images / iStock: eurobanks (b). Shutterstock.com: Antracit (tc). 6-7 Getty Images / iStock: Roman Kulinskiy (t); pepifoto (t/Branch). 6 Alamy Stock Photo: Oleg Zhukov / YAY Media AS (br). Dreamstime.com: Sviatlana Herasimenka (tl). Getty Images / iStock: eurobanks (bc/cliff); Tenny Teng (tc); VectorUp (bc). 7 123RF.com: nikolae (ca). Depositphotos Inc: A7880S (bc). Getty Images / iStock: VectorUp (bl). 8 Getty Images / iStock: SpicyTruffel (cl). 9 Dreamstime.com: Alina Pavlovska (cra). Getty Images / iStock: drmakkoy (ca). 10 Dreamstime.com: Evgenii Naumov (c). 10-11 Getty Images / iStock: StockByM. 11 Getty Images / iStock: Anastasiia Krivenok (tl); SpicyTruffel (cl). 14-15 Dreamstime.com:

Sharpshot (bc). Getty Images / iStock: SeanXu (t). 14 Dreamstime.com: Chanon Tamtad (bl). 15 Alamy Stock Photo: IanDagnall Computing (cl). Getty Images / iStock: HowardOates (ca). 16 123RF.com: madllen (bl). 17 123RF.com: madllen (br). 19 Alamy Stock Photo: Lebrecht Music & Arts (cr). Dreamstime.com: Sergii Kolesnyk (cb); Yuliya Pauliukevich (tc). 20-21 123RF.com: meseberg. 21 Alamy Stock Photo: BOISVIEUX Christophe / hemis.fr (cra); Norman Price (br). Dreamstime.com: Evgenii Naumov (tl). Getty Images / iStock: rasslava (tr). 22 Dreamstime.com: Fotokon (cb); Daniil Lipin (crb). 22-23 Dreamstime.com: Uros Ravbar (b). 23 Dreamstime.com: Drawlab19 (c). Shutterstock.com: delcarmat (br). 24 Dreamstime.com: Viacheslav Dubrovin (clb). Getty Images / iStock: marrio31 (br). 24-25 123RF.com: Vadym Kurgak. Dorling Kindersley: Zishan Mohd (Mermaids). 25 123RF.com: teodora1 (br). Dreamstime.com: Evgenii Naumov (fbr). Getty Images / iStock: A Mokhtari (crb). 26 Alamy Stock Photo: Historic Illustrations / PhotoStock-Israel (bc). 27 Dreamstime.com: Ian Good (bl). Getty Images / iStock: drmakkoy (crb). 28-29 Dreamstime.com: Glanum (c); Honourableandbold (t). Shutterstock.com: delcarmat (b). 30 Dreamstime.com: Nejron (tc). 30-31 Dreamstime.com: Anna Cinaroglu (c); Corey A Ford (c); Subbotina (c/Sand); Sombra12 (cb). Getty Images / iStock: tiler84 (ca). 31 Dreamstime.com: Foto8tik (cb); Jose Gil (t). 32 Alamy Stock Photo: AsiaDreamPhoto (clb). Getty Images / iStock: JDawnInk (b/Fish). 33 Dreamstime.com: Sabelskaya (br). Getty Images / iStock: 26ISO (cr); eurobanks (b). 34-35 123RF.com: Iga Khoroshunova. Dreamstime.com: Refluo (tl). 35 Getty Images / iStock: marrio31 (c). 36-37 Dreamstime.com: Subbotina (b). 37 Alamy Stock Photo: Pictorial Press Ltd (crb). Dreamstime.com: Elena Babenkova (bc); Lefteris Papaulakis (tr); Tuan Nguyen (cra). 38 Alamy Stock Photo: Roop Dey (bl). 39 Alamy Stock Photo: Roberto Fumagalli (clb). Dreamstime.com: Deep Chand (cra). Getty Images / iStock: Travel

Wild (ca). 40 Dreamstime.com: Julia Faranchuk (clb); Dmytro Parkheta; Kseniia Polishchuk (cra). 40-41 Dreamstime.com: Volodymyr Byrdyak (b). 41 Dreamstime.com: Stas11 (tl, ca). Shutterstock.com: First Step Studio (tc). 42 Dreamstime.com: Alina Pavlovska (br). 43 Dreamstime.com: Sabelskaya (c). Getty Images / iStock: eurobanks (cl); pclark2 (tr); JDawnInk (br). 44-45 Dreamstime.com: Altitudevs (Scene); Dewins. 45 Alamy Stock Photo: Matthijs Kuijpers (tr). Dreamstime.com: Marek Uliasz (br). Getty Images / iStock: CTRd (clb). Shutterstock.com: SaveJungle (crb). 46-47 123RF.com: Iga Khoroshunova (b). 47 Getty Images / iStock: DNY59 (crb). 48-49 Dreamstime.com: Photomo (t). 50 Dorling Kindersley: NASA (cla). 52 Dreamstime.com: Denis Kroytor (t). Shutterstock.com: Youssef Mamdouh (l); plutmaverick (cl, cr). 52-53 Dreamstime.com: Estelle30 (cb); Emre Yildiz (t). 53 Dreamstime.com: Ke77kz (b). Shutterstock.com: Youssef Mamdouh (r). 54 Dorling Kindersley: NASA (tr). 55 Getty Images: Sanford / Agliolo (ca). 56-57 Getty Images / iStock: Astrolounge (b). 57 Dreamstime.com: Volodymyr Byrdyak (br). Getty Images / iStock: sansubba (cla). 58 123RF.com: martm (tl). Dreamstime.com: Chernetskaya (crb/leaf). Fotolia: Olena Pantiukh (crb). Getty Images / iStock: AlexRaths (bl, br); Nattawut Sakit (cra); kritdarat Atsadayuttmetee (c). 58-59 123RF.com: teodora1. 59 123RF.com: Karandaev (cl/Coconut). Dreamstime.com: Chernetskaya (cl). 60 Dorling Kindersley: NASA (ca). 61 Dorling Kindersley: Jerry Young (bl). Getty Images / iStock: Jamesmcq24 (cb). 63 Dreamstime.com: insima (tr); Lucie Petrikova (t). 64-65 Dreamstime.com: Subin Pumsom (t). 64 Dorling Kindersley: Barnabas Kindersley (br). Dreamstime.com: Rodho (cb). 65 Dorling Kindersley: Barnabas Kindersley (br). Dreamstime.com: Newlight (bc); Erica Schroeder / Stelya (tl). Getty Images / iStock: A Digit (bl). 67 Dreamstime.com: Olgakotsareva (br). Getty Images / iStock: blueringmedia (c). Getty Images: Fuse (bl); Christian Kaeppke (tr).